W9-BLZ-932

Simple 1-2-3™

Holiday

Publications International, Ltd.

Favorite Brand Name Recipes at www.fbnr.com

Copyright © 2006 Publications International, Ltd.
All rights reserved. This publication may not be reproduced or quoted in whole or in part by any means whatsoever without written permission from:

Louis Weber, CEO
Publications International, Ltd.
7373 North Cicero Avenue
Lincolnwood, IL 60712

Permission is never granted for commercial purposes.

Favorite Brand Name and *Simple 1-2-3* are trademarks of Publications International, Ltd.

All recipes and photographs that contain specific brand names are copyrighted by those companies and/or associations, unless otherwise specified. All photographs *except* those on pages 46, 51, 78, 85, 95, 97, 100, 102, 109, 129 and 142 copyright © Publications International, Ltd.

DOLE® is a registered trademark of Dole Food Company, Inc.

Carnation, Libby's, Nestlé and Toll House are registered trademarks of Nestlé.

Pillsbury is a trademark of The Pillsbury Company, used under license.

SUNKIST is a registered trademark of Sunkist Growers, Inc.

CRISCO® Butter Flavor Shortening and CRISCO® Butter Flavor No-Stick Cooking Spray are artificially flavored.

Some of the products listed in this publication may be in limited distribution.

Front cover photography and photography on pages 61, 62 and 81 by Proffitt Photography Ltd., Chicago.

Pictured on the front cover *(clockwise from bottom left):* Bourbon-Laced Sweet Potato Pie *(page 113),* Country-Style Mashed Potatoes *(page 64),* Steamed Broccoli & Carrots *(page 62),* Turkey with Sausage & Cornbread Stuffing *(page 80)* and Honey Cranberry Sauce *(page 61).*

Pictured on the back cover *(clockwise from top):* Carrie's Sweet Potato Casserole *(page 54),* Coconut Bonbons *(page 141)* and Mini Chick-Pea Cakes *(page 4).*

ISBN-13: 978-1-4127-2324-4
ISBN-10: 1-4127-2324-8

Library of Congress Control Number: 2006900097

Manufactured in China.

8 7 6 5 4 3 2 1

Microwave Cooking: Microwave ovens vary in wattage. Use the cooking times as guidelines and check for doneness before adding more time.

Preparation/Cooking Times: Preparation times are based on the approximate amount of time required to assemble the recipe before cooking, baking, chilling or serving. These times include preparation steps such as measuring, chopping and mixing. The fact that some preparations and cooking can be done simultaneously is taken into account. Preparation of optional ingredients and serving suggestions is not included.

Contents

Sparkling Starters

Mini Chick-Pea Cakes

1 can (15 ounces) chick-peas (garbanzo beans), rinsed and drained
1 cup shredded carrots
⅓ cup seasoned dry bread crumbs
¼ cup creamy Italian salad dressing
1 egg

1. Preheat oven to 375°F. Spray baking sheet with nonstick cooking spray.

2. Mash chick-peas coarsely in medium bowl with hand potato masher. Stir in carrots, bread crumbs, salad dressing and egg; mix well.

3. Shape chick-pea mixture into small patties, using about 1 tablespoon mixture for each. Place on prepared baking sheet.

4. Bake 15 to 18 minutes or until chick-pea cakes are lightly browned on both sides, turning halfway through baking time. Serve warm with additional salad dressing for dipping, if desired.   *Makes about 2 dozen cakes*

Saucy Mini Franks

½ cup *French's®* Sweet & Tangy Honey Mustard

½ cup chili sauce or ketchup

½ cup grape jelly

1 tablespoon *Frank's® RedHot®* Original Cayenne Pepper Sauce

1 pound mini cocktail franks or 1 pound cooked meatballs

1. Combine mustard, chili sauce, grape jelly and *Frank's RedHot* Sauce in saucepan.

2. Add cocktail franks. Simmer and stir 5 minutes or until jelly is melted and franks are hot.

Makes about 6 servings

Prep Time: *5 minutes*
Cook Time: *5 minutes*

Sparkling Starters

Bacon-Wrapped Breadsticks

1. Cut bacon slices in half lengthwise. Wrap half slice of bacon diagonally around each breadstick. Combine Parmesan cheese and parsley, if desired, in shallow dish; set aside.

2. Place 4 breadsticks on double layer of paper towels in microwave oven. Microwave on HIGH 2 to 3 minutes or until bacon is cooked through. Immediately roll breadsticks in Parmesan mixture to coat. Repeat with remaining breadsticks.

Makes 16 breadsticks

8 slices bacon
16 garlic-flavored breadsticks (about 8 inches long)
¾ cup grated Parmesan cheese
2 tablespoons chopped fresh parsley (optional)

Hot Buttered Cider

⅓ **cup packed brown sugar**
¼ **cup butter, softened**
¼ **cup honey**
¼ **teaspoon ground cinnamon**
¼ **teaspoon ground nutmeg**
Apple cider or juice

1. Beat brown sugar, butter, honey, cinnamon and nutmeg until well blended and fluffy. Place butter mixture in tightly covered container. Refrigerate up to 2 weeks. Bring butter mixture to room temperature before using.

2. To serve, heat apple cider in large saucepan over medium heat until hot. Fill individual mugs with hot apple cider; stir in 1 tablespoon butter mixture per 1 cup apple cider. Garnish as desired. *Makes 12 servings*

Sparkling Starters

Smoked Salmon Roses

1. Combine cream cheese, horseradish, minced dill and half-and-half in small bowl. Beat until light and creamy.

2. Spread 1 tablespoon cream cheese mixture over each salmon slice. Roll up jelly-roll fashion. Slice each roll in half crosswise. Arrange salmon rolls, cut sides down, on serving dish to resemble roses. Garnish each "rose" by tucking 1 pepper strip and 1 dill sprig in center. *Makes 32 servings*

1 package (8 ounces) cream cheese, softened
1 tablespoon prepared horseradish
1 tablespoon minced fresh dill plus whole sprigs
1 tablespoon half-and-half
16 slices (12 to 16 ounces) smoked salmon
1 red bell pepper, cut into thin strips

Sparkling Starters

1 cup fat-free or reduced-fat sour cream
4 teaspoons dry ranch-style salad dressing mix
¼ cup finely chopped cucumber
¼ cup finely chopped carrot
¼ cup finely chopped red bell pepper
¼ cup finely chopped zucchini
Bell pepper cutouts (optional)
Assorted fresh vegetables, cut up

Christmas Confetti Dip

1. Combine sour cream and dressing mix in medium bowl; mix well. Stir in chopped vegetables; cover. Refrigerate 2 to 3 hours for flavors to blend.

2. Transfer dip to serving bowl. Garnish with bell pepper cutouts. Serve with assorted fresh vegetable dippers.   *Makes 8 (¼-cup) servings*

Dilly of a Dip: Substitute ½ cup finely chopped seeded cucumber for the 1 cup finely chopped vegetables listed above. Stir in 1 to 1½ teaspoons dill weed or dried basil. Makes about 1¾ cups dip.

Fresh Veggie Spread: Beat 12 ounces softened reduced-fat cream cheese in medium bowl until creamy. Beat in enough fat-free or reduced-fat sour cream to make desired consistency for spreading. Stir in 3 to 4 tablespoons each chopped red bell pepper, zucchini and carrot. Stir in 1 to 1½ teaspoons dill weed or dried oregano. Spread on assorted crackers or party rye bread slices. Makes about 2 cups dip.

Quick Veggie Spread: Prepare Fresh Veggie Spread, substituting ¼ cup dry vegetable soup mix for the chopped fresh vegetables. Makes about 1½ cups spread.

Mushroom Bruschetta

1. Preheat broiler. Peel garlic; cut in half. Mince one half; reserve remaining half.

2. Combine mushrooms, bell pepper, green onion, minced garlic, 1½ teaspoons Parmesan cheese, oil, lemon juice, tarragon and thyme in small bowl. Season to taste with salt and pepper.

3. Arrange bread slices on ungreased baking sheet. Broil 4 inches from heat 2 to 3 minutes per side or until lightly browned.

4. Remove baking sheet from broiler; rub tops of bread with cut side of reserved garlic. Spoon about 1 tablespoon mushroom mixture onto each bread slice; sprinkle with remaining 1½ teaspoons Parmesan cheese. Broil 1 to 2 minutes or until cheese is melted. Serve warm. *Makes 2 servings*

1 clove garlic
½ cup chopped fresh
   mushrooms
2 tablespoons chopped red
   bell pepper
1 green onion, thinly sliced
1 tablespoon grated
   Parmesan cheese,
   divided
1 tablespoon olive or
   canola oil
½ teaspoon lemon juice
¼ teaspoon dried tarragon
¼ teaspoon dried thyme
6 slices French bread
   (½ inch thick)

Midnight Moon

1 round (8 ounces) Brie
   cheese
3 tablespoons plus
   1½ teaspoons
   crumbled blue cheese
2 tablespoons plus
   1½ teaspoons coarsely
   chopped walnuts
3 tablespoons apricot
   preserves, divided
   Assorted crackers

1. Preheat oven to 400°F. Cut Brie cheese horizontally in half. Combine blue cheese and walnuts in small bowl. Spread 4½ teaspoons apricot preserves on cut side of one half of Brie cheese; sprinkle with half of blue cheese-walnut mixture. Place remaining half of Brie cheese on top; spread with remaining 4½ teaspoons apricot preserves.

2. Wrap 3-inch-high strip of foil tightly around Brie; secure with piece of tape. Place in 8-inch square baking pan. Sprinkle remaining blue-cheese-walnut mixture over half of apricot preserves to form crescent moon shape.

3. Bake 7 to 9 minutes or until soft and beginning to melt. Serve immediately with crackers. *Makes 8 servings*

Sparkling Starters

Cranberry Sangría

1. Combine wine, cranberry juice cocktail, orange juice, liqueur, if desired, orange and lime slices in large glass pitcher. Chill 2 to 8 hours before serving.

2. Pour into glasses; add citrus slices from sangría to each glass.

Makes about 7 cups (10 to 12 servings)

Sparkling Sangría: Just before serving, tilt pitcher and gradually add 2 cups well-chilled sparkling water or club soda. Makes about 9 cups, or 12 to 15 servings.

1 bottle (750 mL) Beaujolais or dry red wine
1 cup cranberry juice cocktail
1 cup orange juice
½ cup cranberry-flavored liqueur (optional)
1 orange,* thinly sliced
1 lime,* thinly sliced

*The orange and lime can be scored before slicing to add a special touch. To score, make a lengthwise groove in the fruit with a citrus stripper. Continue to make grooves ¼ to ½ inch apart until the entire fruit has been grooved.

French-Style Pizza Bites (Pissaladière)

2 tablespoons olive oil
1 medium onion, thinly sliced
1 medium red bell pepper, cut into strips
2 cloves garlic, minced
⅓ cup pitted black olives, cut into thin wedges
1 can (10 ounces) refrigerated pizza crust dough
¾ cup (3 ounces) finely shredded Swiss or Gruyère cheese

1. Position oven rack to lowest position. Preheat oven to 425°F. Grease large baking sheet.

2. Heat oil in medium skillet over medium heat until hot. Add onion, bell pepper and garlic. Cook and stir 5 minutes or until vegetables are crisp-tender. Stir in olives; remove from heat.

3. Pat dough into 16×12-inch rectangle on prepared baking sheet.

4. Arrange vegetables over dough; sprinkle with cheese. Bake 10 minutes. Loosen crust from baking sheet; slide crust onto oven rack. Bake 3 to 5 minutes or until golden brown.

5. Slide baking sheet back under crust to remove crust from rack. Transfer to cutting board. Cut dough crosswise into eight 1¾-inch-wide strips. Cut dough diagonally into ten 2-inch-wide strips, making diamond pieces. Serve immediately. *Makes about 24 servings (2 diamonds per serving)*

Crostini

1. Preheat oven to 400°F. Slice baguette into 16 very thin, diagonal slices. Slice each tomato vertically into four ¼-inch slices.

2. Place baguette slices on ungreased nonstick baking sheet. Top each with 1 tablespoon cheese, then 1 slice tomato. Bake about 8 minutes or until bread is lightly toasted and cheese is melted. Remove from oven; top each crostini with about ½ teaspoon pesto sauce. Serve warm.

Makes 8 appetizer servings

¼ **loaf whole wheat baguette (4 ounces)**
4 **plum tomatoes**
1 **cup (4 ounces) shredded part-skim mozzarella cheese**
3 **tablespoons prepared pesto sauce**

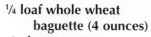

Sparkling Starters

Holiday Shrimp Mold

4½ teaspoons unflavored gelatin
¼ cup cold water
1 can (10¾ ounces) condensed tomato soup, undiluted
1 (3-ounce) package cream cheese
1 cup mayonnaise
1 (6-ounce) bag frozen small shrimp, thawed
¾ cup finely chopped celery
2 tablespoons grated onion
¼ teaspoon salt
White pepper to taste

1. Dissolve gelatin in cold water in small bowl; set aside. Grease four 1-cup holiday mold pans or one 5½-cup holiday mold pan; set aside.

2. Heat soup in medium saucepan over medium heat until hot. Add cream cheese; blend well. Add gelatin mixture, mayonnaise, shrimp, celery, onion, salt and pepper. Pour into prepared molds; refrigerate 30 minutes. Cover with foil and refrigerate overnight.

3. Unmold and serve with assorted crackers. *Makes 12 servings*

Sparkling Starters

Mocha Nog

1. Heat eggnog and coffee granules in large saucepan over medium heat until mixture is hot and coffee granules are dissolved; do not boil. Remove from heat; stir in coffee liqueur.

2. Pour eggnog into individual mugs. Top with whipped cream, if desired.

Makes 8 servings

1 quart eggnog
1 tablespoon instant French vanilla or regular coffee granules
¼ cup coffee-flavored liqueur
Whipped cream (optional)

Sparkling Starters

Mexican Shrimp Cocktail

½ cup WISH-BONE® Italian
Dressing*
½ cup chopped tomato
1 can (4 ounces) chopped
green chilies, undrained
¼ cup chopped green onions
1½ teaspoons honey
¼ teaspoon hot pepper
sauce
1 pound medium shrimp,
cleaned and cooked
2 teaspoons finely chopped
coriander (cilantro) or
parsley

*Also terrific with WISH-BONE®
Robusto Italian or Just 2 Good! Italian
Dressing.

1. In medium bowl, combine Italian dressing, tomato, chilies, green onions, honey and hot pepper sauce. Stir in shrimp.

2. Cover and marinate in refrigerator, stirring occasionally, at least 2 hours. Just before serving, stir in coriander. *Makes about 6 servings*

Sparkling Starters

Pesto-Stuffed Mushrooms

1. Preheat oven to 400°F. Twist off mushroom stems; reserve for another use. Place mushroom caps, stem side up, on ungreased baking sheet.

2. Combine pesto, Parmesan cheese, red pepper, breadcrumbs and pine nuts in small bowl; stir until well blended.

3. Fill mushroom caps with pesto mixture. Sprinkle with mozzarella cheese. Bake 8 to 10 minutes or until filling is hot and cheese is melted. Serve immediately. *Makes 12 mushrooms*

12 medium mushrooms
⅔ cup prepared basil pesto
¼ cup (1 ounce) grated Parmesan cheese
¼ cup chopped roasted red pepper
3 tablespoons seasoned breadcrumbs
3 tablespoons pine nuts
¼ cup (1 ounce) shredded mozzarella cheese

Holiday Star

Topping
- ¾ cup sour cream
- ½ cup mayonnaise
- 2 tablespoons heavy cream
- 1 teaspoon balsamic vinegar
- ¼ cup chopped fresh cilantro
- ¼ cup chopped fresh basil
- ¼ cup chopped roasted red pepper, drained and patted dry
- ½ teaspoon garlic powder
- ¼ teaspoon salt
- Black pepper to taste

Star
- 2 cans (8 ounces each) refrigerated crescent roll dough

Garnishes
- Red bell pepper, chopped
- Green onion, chopped
- Black olive slices

1. Preheat oven to 375°F.

2. For topping, combine sour cream, mayonnaise, cream and vinegar in medium bowl. Stir in cilantro, basil and red pepper. Add garlic powder, salt and black pepper; mix well. Cover; refrigerate at least 1 hour.

3. For star, place 2-inch round cookie cutter or custard cup in center of ungreased 14-inch pizza pan; set aside. Remove dough from one can; unroll onto waxed paper. Seal perforations by pressing down lightly with fingers. Cut 24 circles with 1½-inch round cookie cutter. Remove excess dough from cut circles; set aside. Repeat with second can.

4. Evenly space five dough circles around outside edge of pizza pan. (These will be the star points.) From each star point, make triangle pattern with rows of slightly overlapping dough circles, working toward cookie cutter in center of pan. Roll excess dough into ball; flatten with hands. Cut more circles as needed to completely fill star.

5. Remove cookie cutter from center of star. Bake 12 to 16 minutes or until light golden brown. Cool completely in pan on wire rack, about 30 minutes.

6. Spread topping over star. Garnish with red bell pepper, green onion and black olive slices. Place decorative candle in center of star, if desired. Serve immediately. *Makes about 16 servings*

Hint: For a festive garnish, hollow out a red or green bell pepper and fill it with any remaining dip. Place fresh vegetables, such as broccoli florets or bell pepper strips, around the star.

Sparkling Starters

Easy Spinach Appetizer

1. Preheat oven to 350°F. Melt butter in 13×9-inch baking pan.

2. Beat eggs in medium bowl. Add milk, flour, baking powder and salt; beat until well blended. Stir in spinach, cheese and bell pepper; mix well. Spread mixture over melted butter in pan.

3. Bake 40 to 45 minutes or until set. Let stand 10 minutes; cut into triangles or squares to serve.   *Makes about 3 dozen pieces*

Tip: This appetizer can also be made ahead, frozen and reheated. After baking, cool completely and cut into squares. Transfer squares to baking sheet; place baking sheet in freezer until squares are frozen solid. Transfer to large resealable food storage bag. To serve, reheat squares in preheated 325°F oven for 15 minutes.

2 tablespoons butter
3 eggs
1 cup milk
1 cup all-purpose flour
1 teaspoon baking powder
1 teaspoon salt
2 packages (10 ounces each) frozen chopped spinach, thawed and well drained
4 cups (16 ounces) shredded Monterey Jack cheese
½ cup diced red bell pepper

Hollyberry Fruit Dip

1. In small bowl with wire whisk or mixer at medium speed, beat cream cheese, corn syrup and sugar until fluffy. Blend in sour cream. Fold in cranberries and orange peel.

2. Chill.

3. Serve with fresh fruit dippers or shortbread cookies.

Makes about 2¼ cups dip

Prep Time: *10 minutes, plus chilling*

1 tub (8 ounces) softened cream cheese
½ cup KARO® Light Corn Syrup
2 tablespoons sugar
½ cup light sour cream
1 cup cranberries, chopped
1 tablespoon grated orange peel

Tuscan White Bean Crostini

1. Combine beans, bell pepper and onion in large bowl.

2. Whisk together vinegar, parsley, oil, garlic, oregano and black pepper in small bowl. Pour over bean mixture; toss to coat. Cover; refrigerate 2 hours or overnight.

3. Arrange bread slices in single layer on large ungreased nonstick baking sheet or broiler pan. Broil, 6 to 8 inches from heat, 30 to 45 seconds or until bread slices are lightly toasted. Cool completely.

4. Top each toasted bread slice with about 3 tablespoons bean mixture.

Makes 6 servings

2 cans (15 ounces each) white beans (such as Great Northern or cannellini), rinsed and drained

½ large red bell pepper, finely chopped *or* ⅓ cup finely chopped roasted red bell pepper

⅓ cup finely chopped onion

⅓ cup red wine vinegar

3 tablespoons chopped fresh parsley

1 tablespoon olive oil

2 cloves garlic, minced

½ teaspoon dried oregano

¼ teaspoon black pepper

18 slices French bread, about ¼ inch thick

Shrimp Paté

½ pound cooked peeled shrimp

¼ cup (½ stick) unsalted butter, cut into chunks

2 teaspoons dry vermouth or chicken broth

1 teaspoon lemon juice

1 teaspoon Dijon mustard

¼ teaspoon salt

¼ teaspoon ground mace

⅛ teaspoon ground red pepper

⅛ teaspoon black pepper

½ cup chopped pistachio nuts

2 large heads Belgian endive

1. Combine shrimp, butter, vermouth, lemon juice, mustard, salt, mace, red pepper and black pepper in blender or food processor. Process until smooth. Gently form mixture into 8-inch log on waxed paper. If mixture is too soft to handle refrigerate 1 hour.

2. Spread pistachio nuts on sheet of waxed paper. Roll paté log in nuts to coat. Cover and refrigerate 1 to 3 hours. Separate endive into individual leaves and serve with shrimp log. *Makes 12 (2-tablespoon) servings*

Variation: Spoon shrimp paté into serving bowl and sprinkle with pistachio nuts.

Sparkling Starters

Holiday Cheese Tree

1. Combine cream cheese, Cheddar cheese, red bell pepper, onion, lemon juice and Worcestershire sauce in medium bowl; stir until well blended. Shape into 6-inch-tall cone shape in center of serving plate. Press parsley evenly onto cheese tree.

2. Using cookie cutters or sharp knife, cut yellow bell pepper into desired shapes. Press bell pepper and tomatoes onto tree.

3. Preheat oven to 325°F. Split pita breads in half horizontally. Using 3-inch cookie cutters, cut pita breads into star, tree and bell shapes. Place in single layer on baking sheet. Lightly brush with oil; sprinkle evenly with Parmesan cheese. Bake 15 to 20 minutes or until crisp. Remove to wire racks; cool completely.

Makes about 5 cups dip and 4 dozen cutouts (14 to 16 appetizer servings)

Note: Use kitchen scissors to easily split pita breads in half.

1 package (8 ounces) cream cheese, softened
2 cups (8 ounces) shredded Cheddar cheese
3 tablespoons finely chopped red bell pepper
3 tablespoons finely chopped onion
1 tablespoon lemon juice
2 teaspoons Worcestershire sauce
¾ cup chopped fresh parsley
Yellow bell pepper
Cherry tomatoes, halved
6 pita breads (optional)
Olive oil (optional)
¼ cup grated Parmesan cheese (optional)

Raspberry Wine Punch

1 package (10 ounces) frozen red raspberries in syrup, thawed
1 bottle (750 mL) white Zinfandel or blush wine
¼ cup raspberry-flavored liqueur
Empty half-gallon milk or juice carton
3 to 4 cups distilled water, divided
Sprigs of pine and tinsel
Fresh cranberries

1. Process raspberries with syrup in food processor or blender until smooth. Press through strainer; discard seeds. Combine wine, raspberry purée and liqueur in pitcher; refrigerate until serving time. Rinse out wine bottle and remove label.

2. Fully open top of carton. Place wine bottle in center of carton. Tape bottle securely to carton so bottle will not move when adding water. Pour 2 cups distilled water into carton. Carefully push pine sprigs, cranberries and tinsel into water between bottle and carton to form decorative design. Add remaining water to almost fill carton. Freeze until firm, 8 hours or overnight.

3. Just before serving, peel carton from ice block. Using funnel, pour punch back into wine bottle. Wrap bottom of ice block with white cotton napkin or towel to hold while serving. *Makes 8 servings*

Note: Punch can also be served in punch bowl if desired.

Sparkling Starters

Easiest Three-Cheese Fondue

1. Heat margarine in small saucepan over medium heat until melted. Add onion and garlic; cook and stir 2 to 3 minutes or until tender. Stir in flour; cook 2 minutes, stirring constantly.

2. Stir milk into saucepan; bring to a boil. Boil, stirring constantly, about 1 minute or until thickened. Reduce heat to low. Add cheeses; cook and stir until melted. Stir in red pepper and pepper sauce. Pour fondue into serving dish. Serve with breadsticks and assorted fresh vegetables for dipping.

Makes 8 (3-tablespoon) servings

Lighten Up: To reduce the total fat in this recipe, replace the Cheddar cheese and cream cheese with reduced-fat Cheddar and cream cheeses.

1 tablespoon margarine
¼ cup finely chopped onion
2 cloves garlic, minced
1 tablespoon all-purpose flour
¾ cup reduced-fat (2%) milk
2 cups (8 ounces) shredded mild or sharp Cheddar cheese
1 package (3 ounces) cream cheese, cut into cubes
½ cup (2 ounces) crumbled blue cheese
⅛ teaspoon ground red pepper
4 to 6 drops hot pepper sauce
Breadsticks and assorted fresh vegetables

Black Bean Quesadillas

Nonstick cooking spray
4 (8-inch) flour tortillas
¾ cup (3 ounces) shredded Monterey Jack or Cheddar cheese
½ cup canned black beans, rinsed and drained
2 green onions with tops, sliced
¼ cup chopped fresh cilantro
½ teaspoon ground cumin
½ cup salsa
2 tablespoons plus 2 teaspoons sour cream
Chopped fresh cilantro

1. Preheat oven to 450°F. Spray large nonstick baking sheet with nonstick cooking spray. Place 2 tortillas on prepared baking sheet; sprinkle each with half the cheese.

2. Combine beans, green onions, cilantro and cumin in small bowl; mix lightly. Spoon bean mixture evenly over cheese; top with remaining tortillas. Spray tops with cooking spray.

3. Bake 10 to 12 minutes or until cheese is melted and tortillas are lightly browned. Cut into quarters; top each tortilla wedge with 1 tablespoon salsa and 1 teaspoon sour cream. Transfer to serving plate. Garnish with chopped fresh cilantro.

Makes 8 servings

Sparkling Starters

Holiday Citrus Punch

1. Line 9-inch square baking dish with parchment paper. Spread ice cream evenly in prepared dish; freeze until firm. Meanwhile, place baking sheet in freezer to chill.

2. Remove ice cream from baking dish. Using cookie cutters, cut out desired shapes from ice cream. Transfer cutouts to chilled baking sheet. Press raspberry into center of each cutout; freeze until ready to serve.

3. Combine lemonade and juice concentrates, water and lime juice in punch bowl. Just before serving, add ginger ale. Float ice cream cutouts in punch.

Makes 24 to 26 servings

1 pint vanilla ice cream, softened
   Fresh or frozen raspberries
1 can (12 ounces) frozen lemonade concentrate, thawed
1 can (12 ounces) frozen orange-cranberry juice concentrate, thawed
1 can (12 ounces) frozen Ruby Red grapefruit juice concentrate, thawed
2 cups cold water
¼ cup lime juice
2 bottles (28 ounces each) ginger ale, chilled

Festive Soups & Salads

Double Corn & Cheddar Chowder

1 tablespoon butter
1 cup chopped onion
2 tablespoons all-purpose flour
2½ cups fat-free reduced-sodium chicken broth
1 can (16 ounces) cream-style corn
1 cup frozen whole kernel corn
½ cup finely diced red bell pepper
½ teaspoon hot pepper sauce
¾ cup (3 ounces) shredded sharp Cheddar cheese
Black pepper

1. Melt butter in large saucepan over medium heat. Add onion; cook and stir 5 minutes. Sprinkle onion with flour; cook and stir 1 minute.

2. Add chicken broth; bring to a boil, stirring frequently. Add cream-style corn, corn kernels, bell pepper and hot pepper sauce; bring to a simmer. Cover; simmer 15 minutes.

3. Remove from heat; gradually stir in cheese until melted. Ladle into soup bowls; season to taste with black pepper. *Makes 6 servings*

Vegetable-Chicken Noodle Soup

1 cup chopped celery
½ cup thinly sliced leek
  (white part only)
½ cup chopped carrot
½ cup chopped turnip
6 cups fat-free reduced-
  sodium chicken broth,
  divided
1 tablespoon minced fresh
  parsley
1½ teaspoons fresh thyme *or*
  ½ teaspoon dried
  thyme
1 teaspoon fresh rosemary
  or ¼ teaspoon dried
  rosemary
1 teaspoon balsamic vinegar
¼ teaspoon black pepper
2 ounces uncooked yolk-
  free wide noodles
1 cup diced cooked
  boneless skinless
  chicken breast

1. Combine celery, leek, carrot, turnip and ⅓ cup chicken broth in large saucepan. Cover; cook over medium heat 12 to 15 minutes or until vegetables are tender, stirring occasionally.

2. Stir in remaining 5⅔ cups broth, parsley, thyme, rosemary, vinegar and pepper. Bring to a boil; add noodles. Cook until noodles are tender; stir in chicken. Reduce heat to medium. Simmer until heated through.

Makes 6 servings

Sherried Oyster and Brie Soup

1. Bring sherry to a boil in small saucepan over medium-high heat. Reduce heat to low. Simmer until slightly thickened and reduced to ½ cup. Set aside.

2. Drain oysters, reserving liquor. Set aside.

3. Melt butter in large saucepan over medium-high heat. When foam subsides, stir in mushrooms, shallots and lemon juice; cook and stir 2 minutes. Sprinkle with flour; cook and stir 1 minute more.

4. Add broth and reduced sherry; bring to a boil. Reduce heat to low. Simmer 20 minutes.

5. Cut Brie cheese into wedges; using paring knife, remove and discard outer white rind.

6. Add cheese to soup; stir to melt. Stir in reserved oyster liquor, milk and cream; season to taste with salt and pepper. Heat until very hot. Do not boil.

7. Remove from heat; add oysters. Cover and let stand until oysters are just plumped. Garnish with fresh chives.

Makes 4 servings

1 cup cream sherry
1 quart select Maryland oysters with liquor
2 tablespoons butter
1 pound fresh mushrooms, thinly sliced
½ cup minced shallots
2 tablespoons fresh lemon juice
2 tablespoons all-purpose flour
3 cups beef broth
4 ounces Brie cheese
1 cup milk
1 cup whipping cream
Salt and white pepper
Fresh chives

Golden Tomato Soup

4 teaspoons reduced-calorie margarine

1 cup chopped onion

2 cloves garlic, coarsely chopped

½ cup chopped carrot

¼ cup chopped celery

8 medium Florida tomatoes, blanched, peeled, seeded and chopped

6 cups chicken broth

¼ cup uncooked rice

2 tablespoons tomato paste

1 tablespoon Worcestershire sauce

½ teaspoon dried thyme leaves, crushed

¼ to ½ teaspoon ground black pepper

5 drops hot pepper sauce

1. Melt margarine in large Dutch oven over medium-high heat. Add onion and garlic; cook and stir 1 to 2 minutes or until onion is tender. Add carrot and celery; cook and stir 7 to 9 minutes or until tender. Stir in tomatoes, broth, rice, tomato paste, Worcestershire sauce, thyme, black pepper and hot pepper sauce. Reduce heat to low; cook about 30 minutes, stirring frequently. Remove from heat. Let cool about 10 minutes.

2. In food processor or blender, process soup in small batches until smooth. Return soup to Dutch oven; simmer 3 to 5 minutes or until heated through. Garnish as desired. *Makes 8 servings*

Favorite recipe from **Florida Tomato Committee**

Festive Soups & Salads

White Bean Soup

1. Cook and stir bacon in Dutch oven over medium-high heat about 10 minutes or until crisp.

2. Meanwhile, blend 1½ cans beans and broth in blender or food processor until smooth.

3. Drain all but 1 tablespoon bacon fat from Dutch oven. Stir in onion, garlic, thyme and rosemary. Reduce heat to medium; cover and cook 3 minutes or until onion is transparent. Uncover and cook 3 minutes or until onion is tender, stirring frequently.

4. Add puréed bean mixture and remaining 1½ cans beans to bacon mixture. Cover and simmer 5 minutes or until heated through.   *Makes 4 servings*

Tip: For a special touch, sprinkle chopped fresh thyme over soup just before serving.

6 strips (about 6 ounces) bacon, cut into ½-inch pieces

3 cans (15 ounces each) white beans, drained and rinsed, divided

3 cans (about 14 ounces each) reduced-sodium chicken broth

1 medium onion, finely chopped

3 cloves garlic, minced

1½ teaspoons dried thyme

1½ teaspoons dried rosemary

New England Clam Chowder

1 can (5 ounces) whole
    baby clams, undrained
1 baking potato, peeled
    and coarsely chopped
¼ cup finely chopped onion
⅔ cup evaporated skimmed
    milk
¼ teaspoon white pepper
¼ teaspoon dried thyme
1 tablespoon butter

1. Drain clams, reserving juice. Add enough water to reserved juice to measure ⅔ cup. Combine clam juice mixture, potato and onion in large saucepan. Bring to a boil over high heat; reduce heat and simmer 8 minutes or until potato is tender.

2. Add milk, pepper and thyme to saucepan. Increase heat to medium-high. Cook and stir 2 minutes. Add butter. Cook 5 minutes or until soup thickens, stirring occasionally.

3. Add clams; cook and stir 5 minutes or until clams are firm.

Makes 2 servings

Festive Soups & Salads

Chilly Vichyssoise with Cheese

1. Melt butter in large saucepan over medium heat. Add leeks; cook and stir until limp.

2. Add potatoes and chicken broth to saucepan. Bring to a boil over high heat. Reduce heat to medium-low; simmer, uncovered, 15 minutes or until potatoes are tender.

3. Add cream cheese cubes to potato mixture; melt over low heat, stirring constantly.

4. Process soup in small batches in food processor or blender until smooth. Return soup to saucepan. Stir in milk, half-and-half, salt and pepper.

5. To serve soup hot, cook soup over medium-high heat until bubbly; garnish and serve immediately. To serve soup cold, pour into large bowl; refrigerate at least 6 hours or overnight. Garnish just before serving.   *Makes 8 servings*

2 tablespoons butter
2 small leeks, sliced
4 medium potatoes, peeled and chopped
2 cups chicken broth
1 package (3 ounces) cream cheese, cut into ½-inch pieces, softened
2 cups milk
1 cup half-and-half
½ teaspoon seasoned salt
Dash black pepper
Chopped fresh chives, whole chives and chive flowers for garnish

Roman Spinach Soup

6 cups fat-free reduced-
   sodium chicken broth
1 cup cholesterol-free egg
   substitute
¼ cup minced fresh basil
3 tablespoons freshly grated
   Parmesan cheese
2 tablespoons fresh lemon
   juice
1 tablespoon minced fresh
   parsley
¼ teaspoon white pepper
⅛ teaspoon ground nutmeg
8 cups fresh spinach,
   washed, stemmed and
   chopped
   Fresh lemon slices
   (optional)

1. Bring broth to a boil in 4-quart saucepan over medium heat.

2. Beat together egg substitute, basil, Parmesan cheese, lemon juice, parsley, pepper and nutmeg in small bowl. Set aside.

3. Stir spinach into broth; simmer 1 minute. Gradually pour egg mixture into broth mixture, whisking constantly so egg threads form. Simmer 2 to 3 minutes or until egg is cooked. Garnish with lemon slices. Serve immediately.
Makes 8 servings

Note: Soup may look curdled.

Festive Soups & Salads

Beefy Broccoli & Cheese Soup

1. Bring broth to a boil in medium saucepan. Add broccoli and onion; cook 5 minutes or until broccoli is tender.

2. Meanwhile, brown ground beef in small skillet; drain. Gradually add milk to flour in small bowl, mixing until well blended. Add milk mixture and ground beef to broth mixture; cook, stirring constantly, until mixture is thickened and bubbly.

3. Add cheese and oregano; stir until cheese is melted. Season to taste with salt, pepper and hot pepper sauce.   *Makes 4 to 5 servings*

2 cups chicken broth
1 package (10 ounces) frozen chopped broccoli, thawed
¼ cup chopped onion
¼ pound ground beef
1 cup milk
2 tablespoons all-purpose flour
1 cup (4 ounces) shredded sharp Cheddar cheese
1½ teaspoons chopped fresh oregano *or* ½ teaspoon dried oregano
Salt and black pepper
Hot pepper sauce

1 teaspoon butter
1 large onion, coarsely chopped
1 medium butternut squash (about 1½ pounds), peeled, seeded and cut into ½-inch pieces
2 cans (about 14 ounces each) reduced-sodium or regular chicken broth, divided
½ teaspoon ground nutmeg or freshly grated nutmeg
⅛ teaspoon white pepper
Plain nonfat yogurt and chives (optional)

Butternut Bisque

1. Melt butter in large saucepan over medium heat. Add onion; cook and stir 3 minutes. Add squash and 1 can chicken broth; bring to a boil over high heat. Reduce heat to low; cover and simmer 20 minutes or until squash is very tender.

2. Process squash mixture, in small batches, in food processor until smooth. Return soup to saucepan; add remaining can of broth, nutmeg and pepper. Simmer, uncovered, 5 minutes, stirring occasionally.*

3. Ladle soup into soup bowls. Place yogurt in pastry bag fitted with round decorating tip. Pipe onto soup in decorative design. Garnish with chives.

Makes 6 servings (about 5 cups)

At this point, soup may be covered and refrigerated up to 2 days before serving. Reheat over medium heat, stirring occasionally.

Cream of Butternut Soup: Add ½ cup whipping cream or half-and-half with second can of broth. Proceed as directed.

Turkey, Corn and Sweet Potato Soup

1. In 5-quart saucepan over medium-high heat, cook and stir onion and jalapeño pepper in margarine 5 minutes or until onion is soft. Add broth, potatoes, turkey and salt; bring to a boil. Reduce heat to low; cover and simmer 20 to 25 minutes or until potatoes are tender. Stir in corn. Increase heat to medium and cook 5 to 6 minutes.

2. To serve, spoon 1 cup soup into bowl and garnish with cilantro, if desired.

Makes 8 servings

Favorite recipe from **National Turkey Federation**

½ cup chopped onion
1 small jalapeño pepper,* minced
1 teaspoon margarine
5 cups turkey broth or reduced-sodium chicken broth
1½ pounds sweet potatoes, peeled and cut into 1-inch cubes
2 cups cooked turkey, cut into ½-inch cubes
½ teaspoon salt
1½ cups frozen corn
Fresh cilantro (optional)

Jalapeño peppers can sting and irritate the skin; wear rubber or plastic gloves when handling peppers and do not touch eyes. Wash hands after handling.

Fennel and Potato Bisque

3 tablespoons butter
1 leek, cut into thin slices
3 cups milk
1 tablespoon vegetable
    bouillon granules
½ teaspoon white pepper
⅔ pound fennel bulb with
    1-inch stalk, cut into
    thin slices
2 cups cubed peeled red
    potatoes
1 cup half-and-half
3 tablespoons dry sherry
2 tablespoons all-purpose
    flour
4 ounces blue cheese,
    crumbled
¼ cup plus 2 tablespoons
    finely chopped toasted
    walnuts

1. Melt butter in large saucepan over medium heat. Add leek; cook and stir 10 minutes or until tender.

2. Add milk, bouillon granules and pepper. Bring to a boil over medium-high heat. Add fennel and potatoes. Reduce heat to low. Cover and simmer 15 to 20 minutes or until fennel is very tender.

3. Combine half-and-half, sherry and flour in small bowl; whisk until smooth.

4. Stir flour mixture into fennel mixture. Cook over medium heat until mixture thickens, stirring constantly. Do not boil.

5. Ladle soup into soup bowls; sprinkle each serving evenly with blue cheese and walnuts.

Makes 4 servings

Mesclun Salad with Cranberry Vinaigrette

1. For dressing, whisk together oil, vinegar, mustard, salt and pepper. Stir in cranberries. Cover and chill at least 30 minutes or up to 24 hours before serving.

2. For salad, combine salad greens, goat cheese and walnuts in large bowl. Add dressing; toss well. Transfer to chilled serving plates.

Makes 8 servings

Note: To toast walnuts, place in single layer on ungreased baking sheet. Bake in preheated 350°F oven 8 minutes or until lightly toasted. Cool completely; transfer to airtight container for up to 1 day before serving.

Dressing
- ⅓ **cup extra-virgin olive oil**
- 3 **tablespoons champagne or sherry vinegar**
- 1 **tablespoon Dijon mustard**
- ¾ **teaspoon salt**
- ¼ **teaspoon freshly ground black pepper**
- ½ **cup dried cranberries**

Salad
- 10 **cups (10 ounces) packed mesclun or mixed torn salad greens**
- 4 **ounces goat cheese, crumbled**
- ½ **cup walnuts or pecans, coarsely chopped and toasted**

Market Salad

3 eggs
4 thick slices bacon, crisp-cooked and crumbled
2 cups green beans, cut into 1½-inch pieces, cooked and drained
1 tablespoon minced fresh basil, chives or Italian parsley
4 cups washed mixed baby salad greens
3 tablespoons olive oil
1 tablespoon red wine vinegar
1 teaspoon Dijon mustard
¼ teaspoon salt
¼ teaspoon black pepper

1. Place eggs in small pot with water to cover; bring to a boil over medium-high heat. Immediately remove from heat. Cover; let stand 10 minutes. Drain; cool eggs to room temperature.

2. Combine bacon, green beans, basil and salad greens in large salad bowl. Peel and coarsely chop eggs; stir into salad. Combine oil, vinegar, mustard, salt and pepper in small bowl; drizzle over salad. Toss gently to coat.

Makes 4 servings

Dijon Mustard

Festive Soups & Salads

Mediterranean Orzo Salad

Cook orzo according to package directions, omitting salt. Rinse with cold water and drain well. Mix orzo, bell pepper, cheese, olives and chopped fresh basil in a large bowl. (If using dried basil, add to dressing.) Whisk together salad dressing & seasoning mix, oil, vinegar and sugar. Stir dressing into orzo mixture. Cover and refrigerate at least 2 hours. Garnish with basil leaves before serving, if desired. *Makes 4 to 6 servings*

Salad

- 1 cup orzo pasta
- 1 cup diced red bell pepper
- ½ cup crumbled feta cheese
- 1 can (2¼ ounces) sliced ripe olives, rinsed and drained
- ¼ cup chopped fresh basil *or* ½ teaspoon dried basil
- Fresh basil leaves or parsley sprigs, for garnish (optional)

Dressing

- 1 packet (1 ounce) HIDDEN VALLEY® The Original Ranch® Salad Dressing & Seasoning Mix
- 3 tablespoons olive oil
- 3 tablespoons red wine vinegar
- 1 teaspoon sugar

Festive Soups & Salads

Pasta Primavera Salad

In large bowl, toss pasta with oil; cool. Add remaining ingredients; toss again. Cover; refrigerate at least 2 hours. Just before serving; add additional salad dressing, if desired.

Makes 4 servings

¾ pound uncooked corkscrew pasta, cooked, drained and kept warm
3 tablespoons olive or vegetable oil
2 medium zucchini, cut into ¼-inch slices
1 cup broccoli flowerets, steamed until crisp-tender
1 large red or green bell pepper, cut into small chunks
½ cup cherry tomato halves
⅓ cup sliced radishes
3 green onions, chopped
2 tablespoons drained capers (optional)
1 cup prepared HIDDEN VALLEY® The Original Ranch® Dressing

Festive Soups & Salads

Spinach Salad with Hot Apple Dressing

1. Heat medium nonstick skillet over medium heat until hot. Add bacon and cook 5 to 7 minutes per side or until crisp; remove from pan. Discard drippings. Coarsely chop 3 pieces; set aside. Finely chop remaining 3 pieces; return to skillet. Add apple cider, brown sugar, vinegar and pepper. Heat just to a simmer; remove from heat.

2. Combine spinach, mushrooms, tomato and onion in large bowl. Add dressing; toss to coat. Top with reserved bacon. *Makes 6 servings*

6 strips bacon
¾ cup apple cider
2 tablespoons brown sugar
1 tablespoon plus
   1 teaspoon rice wine
   vinegar
¼ teaspoon black pepper
6 cups washed and torn
   spinach
2 cups fresh sliced
   mushrooms
1 medium tomato, cut into
   wedges
½ cup thinly sliced red
   onion

Bean & Mushroom Salad with Fresh Herb Dressing

½ cup red wine vinegar
2 tablespoons olive oil
1 clove garlic, minced
1 tablespoon chopped fresh oregano
1 tablespoon chopped fresh marjoram
½ teaspoon sugar
⅛ teaspoon black pepper
1 can (16 ounces) red kidney beans, rinsed and drained
1 can (16 ounces) lima beans, rinsed and drained
1 cup sliced mushrooms
1 cup chopped green bell pepper
¼ cup chopped green onions
1 cup cherry tomatoes, halved
10 leaves romaine lettuce (optional)

1. For dressing, combine vinegar, olive oil, garlic, oregano, marjoram, sugar and black pepper in small bowl; mix well.

2. For salad, combine kidney beans, lima beans, mushrooms, bell pepper and onions in large bowl. Add dressing to vegetable mixture; toss to coat. Cover; refrigerate 2 to 3 hours or overnight.

3. Add tomatoes to bean mixture; mix well. Serve on lettuce-lined plates, if desired. *Makes 10 servings*

Veg•All® Vinaigrette Salad

In large mixing bowl, combine Veg•All, beans, tomatoes, green onions and parsley. Pour dressing over vegetable mixture; toss to blend. Cover; refrigerate for at least 2 hours or until chilled. Serve on bed of lettuce.

Makes 4 servings

1 can (15 ounces) VEG•ALL® Original Mixed Vegetables, drained
1 can (15 ounces) black beans, drained and rinsed
1½ cups cherry tomatoes, halved
4 green onions, minced
½ cup minced fresh parsley
1 bottle (8 ounces) Italian salad dressing
Lettuce

Easy Greek Salad

6 romaine lettuce leaves,
   torn into 1½-inch
   pieces
1 medium cucumber,
   peeled and sliced
1 medium tomato,
   chopped
½ cup sliced red onion
⅓ cup crumbled feta cheese
2 tablespoons extra-virgin
   olive oil
2 tablespoons lemon juice
1 teaspoon dried oregano
½ teaspoon salt

1. Combine lettuce, cucumber, tomato, onion and cheese in large serving bowl.

2. Whisk together oil, lemon juice, oregano and salt in small bowl. Pour over lettuce mixture; toss until coated. Serve immediately. *Makes 6 servings*

Serving Suggestion: This simple but delicious salad makes a great accompaniment for grilled steaks or chicken.

Smucker's® Three Bean Salad with Sweet and Sour Apricot Dressing

1. Combine preserves, vinegar and celery seeds in medium salad bowl; stir until well blended.

2. Add kidney beans, green and yellow beans and onion. Toss well to blend. Season with salt and freshly ground black pepper to taste.

Makes 6 servings

½ cup SMUCKER'S® Apricot Preserves
¼ cup red wine vinegar
1 teaspoon celery seeds
1 (16-ounce) can kidney beans, rinsed and drained
¼ pound (1 cup) cooked fresh or frozen green beans, cut into 2-inch pieces
¼ pound (1 cup) cooked fresh or frozen yellow wax beans, cut into 2-inch pieces
1 small red onion, thinly sliced
Salt and black pepper

Winter Pear and Stilton Salad

⅓ cup extra virgin olive oil
1½ tablespoons sherry
    vinegar or white wine
    vinegar
4 teaspoons honey
1 tablespoon Dijon mustard
¼ teaspoon salt
2 ripe Bosc, Bartlett or
    Anjou pears
    Lemon juice (optional)
5 cups assorted gourmet
    mixed salad greens
    (such as oakleaf, frisee,
    watercress, radicchio,
    arugula or escarole),
    torn into bite size
    pieces
2 cups torn Boston or Bibb
    lettuce leaves
1½ cups (6 ounces) Stilton or
    Gorgonzola cheese,
    crumbled
    Black pepper

1. Combine oil, vinegar, honey, mustard and salt in small bowl; stir until well blended. Cover and refrigerate up to 2 days.

2. Cut pears into quarters; remove stem and core. Cut each quarter into ½-inch pieces. To help prevent discoloration, brush pear pieces with lemon juice, if desired.

3. Combine all salad greens in large bowl. Add pears, cheese and dressing. Toss lightly to coat; season to taste with pepper. *Makes 6 to 8 servings*

Italian Antipasto Salad

• In large saucepan, cook artichokes and green beans according to package directions; drain. Rinse under cold water to cool; drain again.

• Place lettuce on serving platter. Arrange cooked vegetables, salami, cheese and peppers in separate piles.

• Drizzle with dressing just before serving.　　*Makes 6 servings*

Prep Time: *5 minutes*
Cook Time: *10 minutes*

Serving Suggestion: Add pitted ripe olives and jarred peperoncini, if desired.

Birds Eye Idea: Don't discard the water after boiling vegetables. Use it for making soups, sauces or rice dishes to keep precious nutrients.

1 box (9 ounces) **BIRDS EYE® frozen Deluxe Artichoke Heart Halves**
1 box (9 ounces) **BIRDS EYE® frozen Deluxe Whole Green Beans**
12 **lettuce leaves**
1 **pound salami, cut into ¾-inch cubes**
¾ **pound provolone cheese, cut into ¾-inch cubes**
1 **jar (7 ounces) roasted red peppers***
⅓ **cup Italian salad dressing**

Or, substitute pimientos, drained and cut into thin strips.

Glorious Side Dishes

Carrie's Sweet Potato Casserole

1 cup packed light brown sugar
½ cup all-purpose flour
⅓ cup butter, melted
3 pounds sweet potatoes, cooked and peeled*
½ cup (1 stick) butter, softened
½ cup granulated sugar
2 eggs, beaten
½ cup evaporated milk
1 teaspoon vanilla
1 cup chopped pecans

For faster preparation, substitute canned sweet potatoes.

1. For topping, combine brown sugar, flour and melted butter in medium bowl; mix well. Set aside. Preheat oven to 350°F. Grease 13×9-inch baking dish.

2. Mash sweet potatoes with softened butter in large bowl. Beat with electric mixer until light and fluffy.

3. Add granulated sugar, eggs, evaporated milk and vanilla, beating after each addition. Spread in prepared dish. Spoon topping over potatoes; sprinkle with pecans.

4. Bake 25 minutes or until set.   *Makes 8 to 12 servings*

Hint: This casserole works well and looks pretty in individual serving dishes. Grease eight 6-ounce oven-proof ramekins and fill almost to the top with sweet potato mixture. Sprinkle with topping and pecans. Bake 20 minutes at 350°F or until set.

Broccoli Supreme

2 packages (10 ounces) frozen chopped broccoli or spinach
1 cup fat-free reduced-sodium chicken broth
2 tablespoons reduced-fat mayonnaise
2 teaspoons instant minced onion (optional)

1. Place broccoli in saucepan. Stir in chicken broth, mayonnaise and onion, if desired. Simmer, covered, stirring occasionally, until broccoli is tender.

2. Uncover; continue to simmer, stirring occasionally, until most of the liquid has evaporated.

Makes 6 servings

Glorious Side Dishes

Southern Pecan Cornbread Stuffing

1. Preheat oven to 350°F. In large bowl, combine stuffing and recipe mix.

2. In 8-inch skillet, melt I Can't Believe It's Not Butter!® Spread over medium heat and cook pecans, stirring occasionally, 5 minutes.

3. Add corn, water, orange juice and pecan mixture to stuffing; toss until moistened. Spoon into 2-quart casserole sprayed with cooking spray.

4. Cover and bake 30 minutes or until heated through. *Makes 8 servings*

Prep Time: *5 minutes*
Cook Time: *35 minutes*

5 cups dry cornbread stuffing mix
1 package KNORR® Recipe Classics™ Leek Soup, Dip and Recipe Mix
½ cup (1 stick) I CAN'T BELIEVE IT'S NOT BUTTER!® SPREAD
1 cup coarsely chopped pecans
1 package (10 ounces) frozen corn, thawed and drained
1 cup hot water
1 cup orange juice

Glorious Side Dishes

Onion-Roasted Potatoes

1 envelope LIPTON®
RECIPE SECRETS®
Onion Soup Mix*
4 medium all-purpose
potatoes, cut into
large chunks (about
2 pounds)
⅓ cup BERTOLLI® Olive Oil

*Also terrific with LIPTON® RECIPE
SECRETS® Onion Mushroom, Golden
Onion or Savory Herb with Garlic
Soup Mix.

1. Preheat oven to 450°F. In 13×9-inch baking or roasting pan, combine all ingredients.

2. Bake uncovered, stirring occasionally, 40 minutes or until potatoes are tender and golden brown.

Makes 4 servings

Prep Time: *10 minutes*
Cook Time: *40 minutes*

Maple-Glazed Carrots & Shallots

1. Place carrots in medium saucepan; add enough water to cover. Bring to a boil over high heat. Reduce heat; simmer 8 to 10 minutes or until carrots are tender. Drain; set aside.

2. In same saucepan, melt butter over medium-high heat. Add shallots; cook and stir 3 to 4 minutes or until shallots are tender and begin to brown. Add carrots, syrup, salt and pepper; cook and stir 1 to 2 minutes or until carrots are coated and heated through.

Makes 4 servings

1 package (16 ounces)
   baby carrots
1 tablespoon butter
½ cup thinly sliced shallots
2 tablespoons maple syrup
¼ teaspoon salt
⅛ teaspoon white pepper

Glorious Side Dishes

Roasted Fall Root Vegetables

½ **pound potatoes**
½ **pound sweet potatoes**
½ **pound carrots**
½ **pound beets**
1 **cup chopped onion**
3 to 4 **cloves garlic, minced**
¼ **cup CRISCO® Pure**
   Canola Oil*
½ **teaspoon dried thyme**
   Salt and pepper to taste

*Or use your favorite Crisco Oil.

1. Heat oven to 350°F.

2. Peel and cut potatoes, sweet potatoes, carrots and beets into ½-inch cubes. Place in large bowl; add remaining ingredients and salt and pepper to taste. Toss to mix well.

3. Place mixture on large ungreased baking sheet; bake for about 25 to 30 minutes or until vegetables can be easily pierced with fork.

Makes 4 to 6 servings

Note: Any variety of root vegetables, such as turnips, parsnips, rutabagas, potatoes, carrots, sweet potatoes, yams or beets, can be used in any combination. Use more or less as desired.

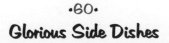
Glorious Side Dishes

Honey Cranberry Sauce

1. Combine cranberries, pineapple with juice, honey, raisins, 2 tablespoons water and allspice in small saucepan. Bring to a boil over medium-high heat. Reduce heat to medium. Cook, uncovered, 3 to 4 minutes or until cranberries pop.

2. Combine remaining 3 tablespoons water and cornstarch in small bowl until smooth. Stir into cranberry mixture. Cook and stir until mixture boils and thickens. Cook and stir 2 minutes more. Garnish with chopped pineapple and raisins.   *Makes 6 servings*

Note: This dish can be served warm or chilled with roast poultry or pork.

1½ cups fresh cranberries
  1 can (8 ounces) pineapple chunks in juice, undrained
  3 tablespoons honey
  2 tablespoons golden raisins or dried currants
  5 tablespoons water, divided
  ¼ teaspoon ground allspice
  1 teaspoon cornstarch
    Chopped pineapple and additional golden raisins (optional)

Steamed Broccoli & Carrots

1 pound broccoli
12 baby carrots*
1 tablespoon butter
Salt and black pepper

*Substitute ½ pound frozen baby carrots or ½ pound regular carrots, cut into 2-inch chunks, for baby carrots.

1. Break broccoli into florets. Discard large stems. Trim smaller stems; cut stems into thin slices.

2. Place 2 to 3 inches of water and steamer basket in large saucepan; bring water to a boil.

3. Add broccoli and carrots; cover. Steam 6 minutes or until vegetables are crisp-tender.

4. Place vegetables in serving bowl. Add butter; toss lightly to coat. Season to taste with salt and pepper.

Makes 4 servings

Baked Eggplant with Cheese

Preheat oven to 375°F. Dip eggplant slices in egg, then into bread crumbs. Heat olive oil in skillet; brown eggplant lightly on both sides. Arrange in buttered baking dish. Season to taste with salt and pepper; sprinkle with parsley and sliced mushrooms. Pour tomato sauce over eggplant. Top with tomato slices and cheese. Sprinkle grated onion over cheese. Bake 30 minutes or until cheese is melted.   *Makes 8 servings*

Favorite recipe from **Wisconsin Milk Marketing Board**

6 or 7 small eggplants, sliced into ½-inch-thick slices
1 egg, beaten
1 cup bread crumbs
2 tablespoons olive oil
   Salt and ground black pepper to taste
1 tablespoon dried parsley
1 can (5 ounces) sliced mushrooms, drained
1 can (15 ounces) chunky tomato sauce
6 thin slices tomato
8 ounces shredded Wisconsin Scamorze or Mozzarella cheese
1 teaspoon grated onion
   Fresh basil leaves for garnish

Glorious Side Dishes

Country-Style Mashed Potatoes

4 pounds baking potatoes, unpeeled and cut into 1-inch pieces

6 large cloves garlic, peeled

½ cup fat-free sour cream

½ cup fat-free (skim) milk, warmed

2 tablespoons butter

2 tablespoons finely chopped fresh rosemary *or* 1 teaspoon dried rosemary

2 tablespoons finely chopped fresh thyme *or* ½ teaspoon dried thyme

2 tablespoons finely chopped fresh parsley

1. Place potatoes and garlic in medium saucepan; cover with water. Bring to a boil. Reduce heat and simmer, covered, about 15 minutes or until potatoes are fork-tender. Drain well.

2. Place potatoes and garlic in large bowl. Beat with electric mixer just until mashed. Beat in sour cream, milk and butter until almost smooth. Stir in rosemary, thyme and parsley.

Makes 8 servings

Glorious Side Dishes

Brussels Sprouts in Mustard Sauce

1. Cut stem from each brussels sprout and pull off outer bruised leaves. Cut an "X" deep into stem end of each brussels sprout. If some brussels sprouts are larger than others, cut large brussels sprouts lengthwise into halves. Bring 2 quarts salted water to a boil in large saucepan. Add brussels sprouts; return to a boil. Boil uncovered 7 to 10 minutes or until almost tender when pierced with fork. Drain. Rinse under cold water; drain thoroughly.

2. Melt butter in same saucepan over medium heat. Add shallots; cook 3 minutes, stirring occasionally. Add half-and-half, mustard, salt and pepper. Simmer 1 minute or until thickened. Add drained brussels sprouts; heat about 1 minute or until heated through, tossing gently with sauce. Sprinkle with cheese, if desired.   *Makes 6 to 8 servings*

1½ pounds fresh brussels sprouts*
1 tablespoon butter
⅓ cup chopped shallots or onion
⅓ cup half-and-half
1 tablespoon plus 1½ teaspoons tarragon Dijon mustard or Dusseldorf mustard
¼ teaspoon salt
⅛ teaspoon black pepper
1½ tablespoons grated Parmesan cheese (optional)

Or, substitute 2 (10-ounce) packages frozen brussels sprouts. Cook according to package directions; drain and rinse as directed.

**Or, substitute 1 tablespoon plus 1½ teaspoons Dijon mustard and ½ teaspoon dried tarragon, for tarragon Dijon mustard.*

Dijon Mustard

Glazed Maple Acorn Squash

1 large acorn or golden
    acorn squash
¼ cup water
2 tablespoons pure maple
    syrup
1 tablespoon butter,
    melted
¼ teaspoon ground
    cinnamon

1. Preheat oven to 375°F.

2. Cut stem and blossom ends from squash. Cut squash crosswise into 4 or 5 equal slices. Discard seeds and membrane. Place water in 13×9-inch baking dish. Arrange squash in dish; cover with foil. Bake 30 minutes or until tender.

3. Combine maple syrup, butter and cinnamon in small bowl; mix well. Uncover squash; pour off water. Brush squash with syrup mixture, letting excess pool in center of squash.

4. Return to oven; bake 10 minutes or until syrup mixture is bubbly.

Makes 4 or 5 servings

Glorious Side Dishes

Tart & Tasty Stuffing

1. Melt butter in medium saucepan over medium heat. Add celery and onion; cook 2 to 3 minutes, or until tender. Stir in thyme and poultry seasoning.

2. Toss together celery mixture, stuffing and broth. Gently stir in cherries. Spoon into lightly greased 2-quart casserole. Bake, covered, in preheated 350°F oven 30 minutes, or until hot.   *Makes 6 servings*

Favorite recipe from **Cherry Marketing Institute**

2 tablespoons butter or margarine

¾ cup chopped celery

½ cup chopped onion

1 teaspoon dried thyme leaves

¼ teaspoon poultry seasoning

1 (7-ounce) package dried herb-seasoned stuffing cubes

¾ cup chicken broth

2 cups frozen unsweetened tart cherries, thawed and drained

Potatoes au Gratin

4 to 6 medium unpeeled baking potatoes (about 2 pounds)
2 cups (8 ounces) shredded Cheddar cheese
1 cup (4 ounces) shredded Swiss cheese
2 tablespoons butter
3 tablespoons all-purpose flour
2½ cups milk
2 tablespoons Dijon mustard
¼ teaspoon salt
¼ teaspoon black pepper

1. Preheat oven to 400°F. Grease 13×9-inch baking dish.

2. Cut potatoes into thin slices. Layer potatoes in prepared dish. Top with cheeses.

3. Melt butter in medium saucepan over medium heat. Stir in flour; cook 1 minute. Stir in milk, mustard, salt and pepper; bring to a boil. Reduce heat and cook, stirring constantly, until mixture thickens. Pour milk mixture over cheese. Cover pan with foil.

4. Bake 30 minutes. Remove foil; bake 15 to 20 minutes or until potatoes are tender and top is brown. Let stand 10 minutes before serving.

Makes 6 to 8 servings

Glorious Side Dishes

Crumb-Topped Snowball

1. Remove and discard leaves and stem from cauliflower. Cut around core with paring knife, being careful not to separate florets from head; remove and discard core. Rinse.

2. Place 1 inch water in large saucepan. Place cauliflower in water, stem side down; cover. Bring to a boil over high heat; reduce heat to low. Simmer 10 to 12 minutes or until crisp-tender; drain. Place cauliflower in 8-inch square baking dish.

3. Preheat oven to 375°F. Melt butter over medium heat in small skillet. Stir in bread crumbs and onions; cook until crumbs are lightly browned. Stir in eggs and lemon juice. Press crumb mixture evenly over top of cauliflower. Place any extra crumb mixture in baking dish. Bake 10 minutes or until crumb mixture is crispy and lightly browned. Garnish as desired. Serve immediately.

Makes 6 servings

1 large head cauliflower
   (about 1¼ pounds)
¼ cup butter
1 cup fresh bread crumbs
   (about 2 slices)
2 green onions, thinly
   sliced
2 eggs, hard cooked and
   finely chopped
2 tablespoons lemon juice

Glorious Side Dishes

Vegetables in Garlic Cream Sauce

1 cup water

4 cups cut-up vegetables such as DOLE® Asparagus, Bell Peppers, Broccoli, Carrots, Cauliflower or Sugar Peas

1 teaspoon olive or vegetable oil

4 cloves garlic, finely chopped

⅓ cup fat free or reduced fat mayonnaise

⅓ cup nonfat or low fat milk

2 tablespoons chopped fresh parsley

• Place water in large saucepan; bring to a boil. Add vegetables; reduce heat to low. Cook, uncovered, 9 to 12 minutes or until vegetables are tender-crisp. Meanwhile, prepare sauce.

• Heat oil in small saucepan over medium heat. Add garlic; cook and stir garlic until golden brown. Remove from heat; stir in mayonnaise and milk.

• Drain vegetables; place in serving bowl. Pour garlic sauce over vegetables; toss to coat evenly. Sprinkle with parsley. *Makes 4 servings*

Prep Time: *10 minutes*
Cook Time: *15 minutes*

Glorious Side Dishes

Baked Spinach Risotto

Preheat oven to 400°F. Grease 1½-quart casserole. Heat oil in 10-inch skillet over medium heat. Add green bell pepper, onion and garlic; cook 5 minutes. Add rice; stir to coat well. Stir in spinach, chicken broth, ¼ cup Parmesan cheese, TABASCO® Green Pepper Sauce and salt. Spoon mixture into prepared baking dish. Sprinkle with remaining ¼ cup Parmesan cheese. Bake 35 to 40 minutes or until rice is tender. *Makes 4 servings*

1 tablespoon olive oil
1 green bell pepper, chopped
1 medium onion, chopped
2 cloves garlic, minced
1 cup arborio rice
3 cups chopped fresh spinach leaves
1 (14½-ounce) can chicken broth
½ cup grated Parmesan cheese, divided
1 tablespoon TABASCO® brand Green Pepper Sauce
1 teaspoon salt

Glorious Side Dishes

Cheese-Stuffed Pattypans

4 pattypan squash (about
    3 inches in diameter)
4 tablespoons butter
2 stalks celery, diced
½ cup chopped onion
½ cup water
1 cup dry herb-seasoned
    stuffing mix
1 cup shredded sharp
    Cheddar cheese

1. Preheat oven to 350°F. Wash pattypans; slice off top above scalloped edge. Discard tops. Scoop out seeds and discard.

2. Place squash shells in large skillet. Pour ¼ inch of water into skillet; cover. Bring to a boil over high heat. Reduce heat to medium-low; simmer 5 minutes. Transfer squash, cut side up, to greased 8×8-inch baking dish.

3. Heat butter in large skillet over medium-high heat until melted and bubbly. Add celery and onion; cook and stir until tender. Add water and stuffing mix. Stir to absorb liquid. Stir in cheese. Divide mixture among squash.

4. Bake 20 to 30 minutes or until squash is fork-tender and stuffing is lightly browned. Garnish as desired. Serve immediately. *Makes 4 servings*

Glorious Side Dishes

Herbed Green Bean Casserole

1. Preheat oven to 350°F.

2. Combine first 9 ingredients in large bowl. Add CRISCO Oil to bread crumb mixture; mix well. Reserve 2 tablespoons bread crumb mixture for top of casserole. Combine green beans and remaining bread crumb mixture in ovenproof dish; sprinkle with reserved crumb mixture.

3. Bake for about 30 minutes or until top is golden and crispy.

Makes 8 servings

Substitution: You can replace the canned beans with frozen or blanched and cooled fresh beans. The dried bread crumbs and herbs can be replaced with Italian-style bread crumbs.

1 cup freshly grated Parmesan cheese
¾ cup dried bread crumbs
2 teaspoons dried basil
2 teaspoons dried parsley
1 teaspoon dried oregano
1 teaspoon garlic powder
½ teaspoon salt
½ teaspoon black pepper
½ teaspoon dried thyme
½ cup CRISCO® Oil*
2 (14-ounce) cans green beans, drained

Use your favorite Crisco Oil.

3 eggs
3 tablespoons all-purpose flour
1 tablespoon sugar
½ teaspoon black pepper
1 can (16½ ounces) cream-style corn
2 cups frozen whole kernel corn, thawed and drained
1 cup (4 ounces) shredded Mexican cheese blend or Monterey Jack cheese
1 jar (2 ounces) diced pimientos, drained
⅓ cup milk

Delicious Corn Soufflé

1. Preheat oven to 350°F. Spray 8-inch round baking dish with nonstick cooking spray. Place dish in oven.

2. Combine eggs, flour, sugar and pepper in large bowl; beat with electric mixer at high speed until smooth. Stir in cream-style corn, corn kernels, cheese, pimientos and milk. Pour into hot baking dish.

3. Bake, uncovered, 55 minutes or until set. Let stand 15 minutes before serving. Garnish as desired. *Makes 6 servings*

Wild Rice with Dried Apricots and Cranberries

1. Rinse wild rice in fine strainer under cold running water. Drain. Combine wild rice, 1½ cups chicken broth and apple juice in 2-quart saucepan. Bring to a boil over medium-high heat. Reduce heat to low; simmer, covered, about 45 minutes or until rice is tender. Drain.

2. Meanwhile, combine white rice and remaining 1½ cups broth in separate 2-quart saucepan. Bring to a boil over medium-high heat. Reduce heat to low; simmer, covered, 12 to 15 minutes.

3. Stir raisins, apricots and cranberries into white rice; simmer 5 minutes or until rice is tender and fluffy and liquid is absorbed. Remove from heat. Let stand covered 5 minutes or until fruit is tender; set aside.

4. Melt butter in large skillet over medium heat. Add onion; cook and stir 5 to 6 minutes until tender. Stir in pecans. Cook and stir 2 minutes.

5. Add wild rice and white rice mixtures to skillet. Stir in parsley; cook and stir over medium heat about 2 minutes or until heated through.

Makes 6 to 8 servings

½ **cup uncooked wild rice**
3 **cups chicken broth, divided**
1 **cup apple juice**
¾ **cup uncooked long-grain white rice**
½ **cup golden raisins**
½ **cup chopped dried apricots**
½ **cup dried cranberries**
2 **tablespoons butter**
¾ **cup chopped onion**
½ **cup coarsely chopped pecans**
⅓ **cup chopped fresh parsley**

Mashed Sweet Potatoes & Parsnips

2 large sweet potatoes (about 1¼ pounds), peeled and cut into 1-inch pieces

2 medium parsnips (about ½ pound), peeled and cut into ½-inch slices

¼ cup evaporated skimmed milk

1½ tablespoons butter

½ teaspoon salt

⅛ teaspoon ground nutmeg

¼ cup chopped fresh chives or green onion tops

1. Combine sweet potatoes and parsnips in large saucepan. Cover with cold water; bring to a boil over high heat. Reduce heat; simmer, uncovered, 15 minutes or until vegetables are tender.

2. Drain vegetables; return to pan. Add milk, butter, salt and nutmeg. Mash potato mixture to desired consistency over low heat. Stir in chives.

Makes 6 servings

Glorious Side Dishes

Old-Fashioned Herb Stuffing

1. Preheat oven to 350°F. Place bread cubes on baking sheet; bake 10 minutes or until dry.

2. Melt butter in large saucepan over medium heat. Add onion, celery and carrot; cover and cook 10 minutes or until vegetables are tender. Add broth, thyme, sage, paprika and pepper; bring to a simmer. Stir in bread pieces; mix well. Remove pan from heat.

3. Coat 1½-quart baking dish with nonstick cooking spray. Spoon stuffing into dish. Cover and bake 25 to 30 minutes or until heated through.

Makes 4 servings

- **6 slices (8 ounces) whole wheat, rye or white bread (or combination), cut into ½-inch cubes**
- **1 tablespoon butter**
- **1 cup chopped onion**
- **½ cup thinly sliced celery**
- **½ cup thinly sliced carrot**
- **1 cup fat-free reduced-sodium chicken broth**
- **1 tablespoon chopped fresh thyme *or* 1 teaspoon dried thyme**
- **1 tablespoon chopped fresh sage *or* 1 teaspoon dried sage**
- **½ teaspoon paprika**
- **¼ teaspoon black pepper**

Glorious Side Dishes

Creamed Spinach á la Lawry's®

2 packages (10 ounces each) frozen spinach, cooked and drained

4 slices bacon

1 small onion, minced

2 cloves garlic, minced

2 tablespoons all-purpose flour

1 teaspoon LAWRY'S® Seasoned Salt

½ teaspoon freshly ground black pepper, or to taste

2 cups milk

Drain spinach well and squeeze out excess moisture with hands; chop finely and set aside. Fry bacon in heavy skillet until crisp; remove, drain and chop. Sauté onion and garlic in bacon drippings; add flour, Lawry's® Seasoned Salt and pepper and blend thoroughly. Slowly add milk, stirring constantly until thickened. Add spinach and bacon; heat.

Makes 4 servings

Prep Time: *15 minutes*
Cook Time: *20 minutes*

Meal Idea: Serve with prime rib or roast beef.

Glorious Side Dishes

Broccoli-Rice Casserole

1. Preheat oven to 350°F. Coat 1½-quart baking dish with nonstick cooking spray; set aside.

2. Coat large skillet with cooking spray. Add onion, celery and bell pepper; cook and stir over medium heat until crisp-tender. Stir in soup and sour cream. Layer rice and broccoli in prepared dish. Top with soup mixture, spreading evenly.

3. Cover and bake 20 minutes. Top with tomato slices, if desired; bake, uncovered, 10 minutes.

Makes 6 servings

Nonstick cooking spray
½ cup chopped onion
½ cup chopped celery
⅓ cup chopped red bell pepper
1 can (10¾ ounces) condensed broccoli and cheese soup, undiluted
¼ cup sour cream
2 cups cooked rice
1 package (10 ounces) frozen chopped broccoli, thawed and drained
Tomato slices (optional)

Merry Main Dishes

Turkey with Sausage & Cornbread Stuffing

1 pound bulk pork sausage
1½ cups chopped onions
1 cup chopped celery
1 clove garlic, minced
1 bag (16 ounces) corn bread stuffing mix
1 can (about 14 ounces) chicken broth
2 teaspoons poultry seasoning
2 tablespoons butter, melted
1 (14- to 16-pound) turkey, thawed

1. Preheat oven to 325°F. Cook and stir sausage in large skillet over medium heat until browned; drain. Add onions, celery and garlic to sausage in skillet; cook and stir about 5 minutes or until vegetables are tender. Stir in stuffing mix, broth and poultry seasoning until blended.

2. Brush butter over outside of turkey. Spoon stuffing into turkey cavity; close with metal skewers. Place turkey, breast side up, on rack in shallow roasting pan. Insert ovenproof meat thermometer into thickest part of thigh not touching bone.

3. Bake turkey uncovered 4 to 5 hours, basting occasionally with pan drippings until temperature reaches 180°F. Let stand 20 minutes before carving. *Makes 10 servings*

Note: If turkey is browning too quickly, tent loosely with foil, being careful not to touch meat thermometer.

Chicken with Kale Stuffing

4 boneless skinless chicken
   breast halves
1 cup sliced mushrooms
½ cup chopped onion
2 tablespoons dry white
   wine
1 teaspoon chopped fresh
   oregano *or* ¼ teaspoon
   dried oregano
1 clove garlic, minced
½ teaspoon black pepper
2 cups chopped stemmed
   washed kale
2 tablespoons light
   mayonnaise
½ cup seasoned bread
   crumbs

1. Preheat oven to 400°F. Coat shallow baking dish with nonstick cooking spray; set aside. Remove fat from chicken. Pound chicken with meat mallet to ½-inch thickness; set aside.

2. Heat skillet over medium-high heat. Add mushrooms, onion, wine, oregano, garlic and pepper; cook and stir about 5 minutes or until onion is softened. Add kale; cook and stir until kale is wilted.

3. Spread kale mixture evenly over flattened chicken breasts. Roll up chicken; secure with toothpicks or metal skewers. Brush chicken with mayonnaise; coat with bread crumbs. Place chicken, seam side down, in prepared baking dish. Bake 25 minutes or until chicken is golden brown and no longer pink near centers. Remove toothpicks before serving. *Makes 4 servings*

Baked Holiday Ham with Cranberry-Wine Compote

1. For compote, heat oil in large saucepan over medium-high heat until hot; add onion and celery. Cook and stir until tender. Stir in wine, honey and sugar; bring to a boil. Add cranberries; return to a boil. Reduce heat to low; cover and simmer 10 minutes. Cool completely.

2. Reserve 1 cup clear syrup from cranberry mixture. Transfer remaining cranberry mixture to small serving bowl; cover and refrigerate.

3. Slice away skin from ham with sharp utility knife. (Omit step if meat retailer has already removed skin.)

4. Preheat oven to 325°F. Score fat on ham in diamond design with sharp utility knife; stud with whole cloves. Place ham, fat side up, on rack in shallow roasting pan.

5. Bake, uncovered, 1½ hours. Baste ham with reserved cranberry-wine syrup. Bake, basting with cranberry-wine syrup twice, 1 to 2 hours more or until meat thermometer inserted into thickest part of ham, not touching bone, registers 140°F, basting with cranberry-wine syrup two more times.*

6. Let ham stand 10 minutes. Transfer to warm serving platter. Slice ham and serve with chilled cranberry wine compote.   *Makes 16 to 20 servings*

*Total cooking time for ham should be 18 to 24 minutes per pound.

2 teaspoons peanut oil
⅔ cup chopped onion
½ cup chopped celery
1 cup red wine
1 cup honey
½ cup sugar
**1 package (12 ounces)
    fresh cranberries**
**1 fully-cooked smoked ham
    (10 pounds)**
Whole cloves

Herb-Roasted Racks of Lamb

½ cup mango chutney, chopped

2 to 3 cloves garlic, minced

2 whole racks (6 ribs each) lamb loin chops (2½ to 3 pounds)

1 cup fresh French or Italian bread crumbs

1 tablespoon chopped fresh thyme *or* 1 teaspoon dried thyme

1 tablespoon chopped fresh rosemary *or* 1 teaspoon dried rosemary

1 tablespoon chopped fresh oregano *or* 1 teaspoon dried oregano

1. Preheat oven to 400°F. Combine chutney and garlic in small bowl; spread evenly over meaty side of lamb. Combine remaining ingredients in separate small bowl; pat crumb mixture evenly over chutney mixture.

2. Place lamb racks, crumb sides up, on rack in shallow roasting pan. Roast 30 to 35 minutes for medium or until internal temperature reaches 145°F when tested with meat thermometer inserted into thickest part of lamb, not touching bone.

3. Remove lamb to cutting board; tent with foil. Let stand 10 to 15 minutes before carving. (Internal temperature will continue to rise 5°F to 10°F during stand time.) Using large knife, slice between ribs into individual chops. Serve immediately.

Makes 4 servings

Cranberry Orange Game Hens with Vegetable Stuffing

1. Preheat oven to 400°F. Remove as much fat as possible from game hens. Combine stuffing mix, carrot, celery and poultry seasoning in medium bowl. Add chicken stock; stir until well blended. Season with salt and pepper. Fill cavity of each hen with stuffing; place in roasting pan. Bake at 400°F for 45 minutes.

2. Meanwhile, combine cranberries, marmalade, water and lemon juice in medium saucepan. Cook over medium-high heat for 5 to 8 minutes or until cranberries have released their juice. Set aside.

3. Remove game hens from oven. Spread sauce over tops and sides of hens. Reserve any extra sauce to serve later with hens. Return hens to oven and continue baking 10 to 15 minutes.

4. To serve, place game hens on 4 serving plates. Spoon additional sauce over hens.

Makes 4 servings

Game Hens
- **4 small Cornish game hens (16 ounces each)**
- **2 cups bread stuffing mix**
- **1 carrot, finely diced**
- **1 stalk celery, finely diced**
- **1 teaspoon poultry seasoning**
- **1 cup chicken stock**
- **Salt and black pepper**

Sauce
- **1 cup fresh or frozen cranberries, chopped**
- **1 cup (12-ounce jar) SMUCKER'S® Sweet Orange Marmalade**
- **¼ cup water**
- **1 teaspoon lemon juice**

1 (4- to 5-pound) boneless pork loin roast
1¼ cups fresh parsley, chopped and divided
½ cup fresh basil leaves, chopped
½ cup pine nuts
½ cup grated Parmesan cheese
6 cloves garlic, peeled and chopped
½ pound ground pork
½ pound Italian sausage
1 cup dry bread crumbs
¼ cup milk
1 egg
1 teaspoon ground black pepper

Stuffed Pork Loin Genoa Style

1. In food processor or blender, process 1 cup parsley, basil, pine nuts, Parmesan cheese and garlic. Set aside.

2. Mix together ground pork, Italian sausage, bread crumbs, milk, egg, remaining ¼ cup parsley and pepper.

3. Place roast fat-side down on cutting board. Spread with the herb-cheese mixture; place ground pork mixture along center of loin. Fold in half; tie with kitchen string. Roast on rack in shallow baking pan at 350°F for 1½ hours or until internal temperature reaches 155°F. Slice to serve.

Makes 10 servings

Prep Time: *15 minutes*
Cook Time: *90 minutes*

Favorite recipe from **National Pork Board**

Merry Main Dishes

Roasted Herb & Garlic Tenderloin

1. Preheat oven to 425°F. To hold shape of roast, tie roast with cotton string at 1½-inch intervals. Place roast on meat rack in shallow roasting pan.

2. Place peppercorns in small heavy resealable plastic food storage bag. Squeeze out excess air; seal bag tightly. Pound peppercorns with flat side of meat mallet or rolling pin until peppercorns are cracked.

3. Combine cracked peppercorns, basil, thyme, rosemary and garlic in small bowl; rub over top surface of roast.

4. Roast 40 to 50 minutes until internal temperature reaches 135°F for medium-rare or 150°F for medium when tested with meat thermometer inserted into the thickest part of roast.

5. Transfer roast to cutting board; cover with foil. Let stand 10 to 15 minutes before carving. Internal temperature will continue to rise 5°F to 10°F during stand time. Remove and discard string. To serve, carve roast crosswise into ½-inch-thick slices with large carving knife. Season to taste with salt and pepper.

Makes 10 to 12 servings

1 beef tenderloin roast, trimmed (3 to 4 pounds)
1 tablespoon black peppercorns
2 tablespoons chopped fresh basil *or*
   2 teaspoons dried basil
4½ teaspoons chopped fresh thyme *or*
   1½ teaspoons dried thyme
1 tablespoon chopped fresh rosemary *or*
   1 teaspoon dried rosemary
1 tablespoon minced garlic
Salt and black pepper

Merry Main Dishes

Crispy Duck

1 whole duck (about
   5 pounds)
1 tablespoon rubbed sage
1 teaspoon salt
¼ teaspoon black pepper
3 cups vegetable oil
1 tablespoon butter
2 large Granny Smith or
   Rome Beauty apples,
   cored and cut into thin
   wedges
½ cup clover honey

1. Remove neck and giblets from duck. Cut wing tips and second wing sections off duck; wrap and freeze for another use. Trim excess fat and excess skin from duck; discard. Rinse duck and cavity under cold running water; pat dry with paper towels. Cut duck into quarters, removing backbone and breast bone.

2. Place duck in 13×9-inch baking dish. Combine sage, salt and black pepper. Rub duck with sage mixture. Cover; refrigerate 1 hour.

3. To steam duck, place wire rack in wok. Add water to 1 inch below rack. (Water should not touch rack.) Cover wok; bring water to a boil over medium-high heat. Arrange duck, skin sides up, on wire rack. Cover; steam 40 minutes or until fork-tender. (Add boiling water to wok to keep water at same level.)

4. Transfer cooked duck to plate. Carefully remove rack from wok; discard water. Rinse wok and dry. Heat oil in wok over medium-high heat until oil registers 375°F on deep-fry thermometer. Add ½ of duck, skin sides down. Fry 5 to 10 minutes or until crisp and golden brown, turning once. Drain duck on paper towels. Repeat with remaining duck, reheating oil.

5. Pour off oil. Melt butter in wok over medium heat. Add apples; cook and stir 5 minutes or until wilted. Stir in honey and bring to a boil. Transfer apples with slotted spoon to warm serving platter. Arrange duck on apples. Drizzle honey mixture over duck.

Makes 4 servings

Roast Turkey Breast with Spinach-Blue Cheese Stuffing

1. Preheat oven to 350°F. Coat roasting pan and rack with nonstick cooking spray.

2. Unroll turkey breast; rinse and pat dry. Place turkey between 2 sheets of plastic wrap or waxed paper. Pound turkey to 1-inch thickness using flat side of meat mallet or rolling pin. Remove and discard skin from one half of turkey breast; turn meat over so skin side (on other half) faces down.

3. Combine spinach, blue cheese, cream cheese, green onions, mustard, basil and oregano in medium bowl; mix well. Spread evenly over turkey breast. Roll up turkey so skin is on top. Tie closed with kitchen string.

4. Carefully place turkey breast on rack; sprinkle with pepper and paprika. Roast 1½ hours or until no longer pink in center of breast. Remove from oven; let stand 10 minutes before removing skin and slicing into 14 (¼-inch-thick) slices.

Makes 14 servings

1 frozen whole boneless turkey breast, thawed (3½ to 4 pounds)
1 package (10 ounces) frozen chopped spinach, thawed and squeezed dry
2 ounces blue cheese or feta cheese
2 ounces cream cheese
½ cup finely chopped green onions
4½ teaspoons Dijon mustard
4½ teaspoons dried basil
2 teaspoons dried oregano
Black pepper
Paprika

Stuffed Chicken with Apple Glaze

1 (3½- to 4-pound) frying chicken
½ teaspoon salt
¼ teaspoon black pepper
2 tablespoons vegetable oil
1 package (6 ounces) chicken-flavored stuffing mix plus ingredients to prepare mix
1 large apple, chopped
½ teaspoon grated lemon peel
¼ cup chopped walnuts
¼ cup raisins
¼ cup thinly sliced celery
½ cup apple jelly
1 tablespoon lemon juice
½ teaspoon ground cinnamon

1. Preheat oven to 350°F. Sprinkle inside of chicken with salt and pepper; rub outside with oil.

2. Prepare stuffing mix in large bowl according to package directions. Add apple, lemon peel, walnuts, raisins and celery to prepared stuffing; mix thoroughly. Stuff body cavity loosely with stuffing.

3. Place chicken in shallow baking pan. Cover loosely with foil; roast chicken 1 hour.

4. For glaze, combine jelly, lemon juice and cinnamon in small saucepan. Simmer over low heat 3 minutes, stirring often, until jelly dissolves and mixture is well blended. Remove foil from chicken; brush with some glaze.

5. Roast chicken, uncovered, brushing frequently with glaze, 30 minutes or until meat thermometer inserted into thickest part of thigh, not touching bone, registers 180°F. Let chicken stand 15 minutes before carving.

Makes 4 servings

Merry Main Dishes

Cranberry-Glazed Ham

1. Preheat oven to 300°F. Place ham in large roasting pan lined with heavy-duty aluminum foil.

2. Combine cranberry sauce, mustard, cinnamon and allspice; mix well. Spread half of mixture evenly over top of ham (glaze will melt and spread as it cooks).

3. Bake 1 hour; spread remaining cranberry mixture over top of ham. Continue to bake until internal temperature of ham reaches 140°F, about 1 hour.

4. Transfer ham to carving board; let stand 5 minutes before serving.

Makes 10 to 12 servings

1 (5- to 6-pound) fully cooked spiral sliced ham half*

¾ cup cranberry sauce or cranberry chutney

¼ cup Dijon or hot Dijon mustard

1 teaspoon ground cinnamon

¼ teaspoon ground allspice

A whole ham is usually 10 to 12 pounds and serves 24. Double glaze ingredients if using a whole ham.

Beef Tenderloin with Roasted Vegetables

1 beef tenderloin roast
   (about 3 pounds),
   trimmed of fat
½ cup chardonnay or other
   dry white wine
½ cup reduced-sodium soy
   sauce
2 cloves garlic, sliced
1 tablespoon fresh
   rosemary
1 tablespoon Dijon mustard
1 teaspoon dry mustard
1 pound small red or white
   potatoes, cut into
   1-inch pieces
1 pound brussels sprouts
1 package (12 ounces)
   baby carrots

1. Place roast in large resealable food storage bag. Combine wine, soy sauce, garlic, rosemary, Dijon mustard and dry mustard in small bowl. Pour over roast. Seal bag; turn to coat. Marinate in refrigerator 4 to 12 hours, turning several times.

2. Preheat oven to 425°F. Spray 13×9-inch baking pan with nonstick cooking spray. Place potatoes, brussels sprouts and carrots in pan. Remove roast from marinade. Pour marinade over vegetables; toss to coat well. Cover vegetables with foil; roast 30 minutes. Stir.

3. Place tenderloin on vegetables. Roast, uncovered, 35 to 45 minutes or until internal temperature of roast reaches 135°F for medium-rare to 150°F for medium when tested with meat thermometer inserted into thickest part of tenderloin.

4. Transfer tenderloin to cutting board; cover with foil. Let stand 10 to 15 minutes before carving. (Internal temperature will continue to rise 5°F to 10°F during stand time.)

5. Stir vegetables; test for doneness. Continue to bake if not tender. Slice tenderloin; arrange on serving platter with roasted vegetables.

Makes 10 servings

Merry Main Dishes

Apple Stuffed Pork Loin Roast

1. Preheat oven to 325°F. Combine garlic, salt, rosemary, thyme and pepper in small bowl. Cut lengthwise down roast almost to, but not through bottom. Open like a book. Rub half of garlic mixture onto cut sides of pork.

2. Melt butter in large skillet over medium-high heat. Add apples and onion; cook and stir 5 to 10 minutes or until soft. Stir in brown sugar and mustard. Spread mixture evenly onto one cut side of roast. Close halves; tie roast with kitchen string at 2-inch intervals. Place roast on rack in shallow roasting pan. Pour apple cider over roast. Rub outside of roast with remaining garlic mixture.

3. Roast, uncovered, basting frequently with pan drippings 2 to 2½ hours or until thermometer inserted into thickest part of roast registers 155°F. Remove roast from oven; let stand 15 minutes before slicing. (Internal temperature will continue to rise 5°F to 10°F during stand time.) Carve roast crosswise to serve. *Makes 14 to 16 servings*

2 cloves garlic, minced
1 teaspoon coarse salt
1 teaspoon dried rosemary
½ teaspoon dried thyme
½ teaspoon black pepper
1 boneless center cut pork loin roast (4 to 5 pounds)
1 tablespoon butter
2 large tart apples, peeled, cored and thinly sliced (about 2 cups)
1 medium onion, cut into thin strips (about 1 cup)
2 tablespoons brown sugar
1 teaspoon Dijon mustard
1 cup apple cider or apple juice

Roast Turkey Breast with Sausage and Apple Stuffing

8 ounces bulk pork sausage
1 medium apple, cored, peeled and finely chopped
1 shallot or small onion, peeled and finely chopped
1 stalk celery, finely chopped
¼ cup chopped hazelnuts
½ teaspoon rubbed sage, divided
½ teaspoon salt, divided
½ teaspoon black pepper, divided
1 tablespoon butter
1 whole boneless turkey breast (4½ to 5 pounds), thawed if frozen
4 to 6 fresh sage leaves (optional)
1 cup chicken broth

1. Preheat oven to 325°F. Crumble pork sausage into large skillet. Add apple, shallot and celery. Cook and stir until sausage is cooked through and apple and vegetables are tender. Stir in hazelnuts, ¼ teaspoon sage, ¼ teaspoon salt and ¼ teaspoon pepper.

2. Mash butter with remaining ¼ teaspoon each sage, salt and pepper. Spread over turkey breast skin. Ease skin over turkey breast and arrange sage leaves under skin, if desired. Spoon sausage stuffing into turkey cavity. Close cavity with metal skewers. Place turkey, skin side down on rack in shallow roasting pan. Pour broth into pan.

3. Roast turkey 45 minutes. Remove turkey from oven, turn skin side up. Baste with broth. Return to oven and roast 1 hour, or until meat thermometer registers 170°F. Remove from oven. Let turkey rest 10 minutes before slicing.

Makes 6 servings

Merry Main Dishes

CURE 81® Ham with Honey Mustard Glaze

Bake ham according to package directions. Meanwhile, combine brown sugar, honey and mustard. Thirty minutes before ham is done, remove from oven. Score surface; spoon glaze over ham. Return to oven and continue basting with glaze during last 30 minutes of baking.

Makes 8 to 10 servings

1 **CURE 81® ham half**
1 **cup packed brown sugar**
½ **cup honey**
2 **tablespoons prepared mustard**

Crab-Stuffed Chicken Breasts

1 package (8 ounces)
   cream cheese, softened
6 ounces frozen crabmeat,
   thawed and drained
1 envelope LIPTON®
   RECIPE SECRETS®
   Savory Herb with
   Garlic Soup Mix
6 boneless, skinless
   chicken breast halves
   (about 1½ pounds)
¼ cup all-purpose flour
2 eggs, beaten
¾ cup plain dry bread
   crumbs
2 tablespoons BERTOLLI®
   Olive Oil
1 tablespoon I CAN'T
   BELIEVE IT'S NOT
   BUTTER!® Spread

1. Preheat oven to 350°F. Combine cream cheese, crabmeat and soup mix; set aside. With knife parallel to cutting board, slice horizontally through each chicken breast, stopping 1 inch from opposite edge; open breasts. Evenly spread each breast with cream cheese mixture. Close each chicken breast, securing open edge with wooden toothpicks.

2. Dip chicken in flour, then eggs, then bread crumbs, coating well. In 12-inch skillet over medium-high heat, heat oil and I Can't Believe It's Not Butter!® Spread; cook chicken 10 minutes or until golden, turning once. Transfer chicken to 13×9-inch baking dish and bake uncovered 15 minutes or until chicken is thoroughly cooked in center. Remove toothpicks before serving.   *Makes about 6 servings*

Serving Suggestion: Serve with a mixed green salad and warm garlic bread.

Merry Main Dishes

Holiday Hens with Sherry Gravy

Preheat oven to 350°F. In large skillet over low heat, melt butter. Stir in lemon juice and Worcestershire sauce. Brush hens with butter mixture; sprinkle with salt and pepper. Tie legs together with kitchen string.

Place hens in large, shallow roasting pan. Roast 1 to 1¼ hours until skin is crisp and golden brown, juices run clear and no hint of pink remains when thigh is pierced. Remove to warm serving platter and discard string. Tie legs with scallion greens; garnish with rosemary.

To prepare sauce, stir flour into pan drippings. Cook over medium-low heat, 4 to 5 minutes until flour is brown, stirring constantly. Gradually whisk in chicken broth and sherry; cook 3 to 4 minutes longer, until gravy is smooth and thickened, stirring often. Strain gravy into a sauce dish and serve with hens.

Makes 8 to 12 servings

4 teaspoons butter or margarine
2 teaspoons lemon juice
1 teaspoon Worcestershire sauce
3 packages (3 pounds each) PERDUE® Fresh Whole Cornish Hens (6 hens)
Salt and ground black pepper to taste
Scallion greens (optional)
6 sprigs fresh rosemary (optional)
3 tablespoons all-purpose flour
1 can (about 14 ounces) chicken broth
½ cup dry sherry

Mustard Crusted Rib Roast

1 (3-rib) beef rib roast,
   trimmed* (6 to
   7 pounds)
3 tablespoons Dijon
   mustard
1 tablespoon plus
   1½ teaspoons chopped
   fresh tarragon *or*
   1½ teaspoons dried
   tarragon
3 cloves garlic, minced
¼ cup dry red wine
⅓ cup finely chopped
   shallots (about
   2 shallots)
1 tablespoon all-purpose
   flour
1 cup beef broth
   Mashed potatoes
   (optional)

*Ask meat retailer to remove chine
bone for easier carving. Trim fat to
¼-inch thickness.*

1. Preheat oven to 450°F. Place roast, bone-side-down, in shallow roasting pan. Combine mustard, tarragon and garlic in small bowl; spread over all surfaces of roast, except bottom. Insert meat thermometer into thickest part of roast, not touching bone or fat. Roast 10 minutes.

2. *Reduce oven temperature to 350°F.* Roast 2½ to 3 hours for medium or until internal temperature reaches 145°F when tested with meat thermometer inserted into thickest part of roast, not touching bone.

3. Transfer roast to cutting board; cover with foil. Let stand 10 to 15 minutes before carving. Internal temperature will continue to rise 5°F to 10°F during stand time.

4. To make gravy, pour drippings from roasting pan, reserving 1 tablespoon in medium saucepan. Add wine to roasting pan; place over 2 burners. Cook over medium heat 2 minutes or until slightly thickened, stirring to scrape up browned bits; set aside.

5. Add shallots to reserved drippings in saucepan; cook and stir over medium heat 4 minutes or until softened. Add flour; cook and stir 1 minute. Add broth and wine mixture; cook 5 minutes or until sauce thickens, stirring occasionally. Pour through strainer into gravy boat, pressing with back of spoon on shallots; discard solids.

6. Carve roast into ½-inch-thick slices. Serve with gravy and mashed potatoes, if desired. *Makes 6 to 8 servings*

Baked Ham with Sweet and Spicy Glaze

1. Preheat oven to 325°F. Place ham, fat side up, on rack in roasting pan. Insert meat thermometer into thickest part of ham away from fat or bone. Roast ham in oven about 3 hours.

2. To prepare glaze, combine brown sugar, vinegar, raisins and peach syrup in medium saucepan. Bring to a boil over high heat; reduce to low and simmer 8 to 10 minutes. In small bowl, dissolve cornstarch in orange juice; add to brown sugar mixture. Add remaining ingredients; mix well. Cook over medium heat, stirring constantly, until mixture boils and thickens. Remove from heat.

3. Remove ham from oven. Generously brush half of glaze over ham; bake 30 minutes longer or until meat thermometer registers 160°F. Remove ham from oven and brush with remaining glaze. Let ham stand about 20 minutes before slicing. *Makes 8 to 10 servings*

1 (8-pound) bone-in smoked half ham
¾ cup packed brown sugar
⅓ cup cider vinegar
¼ cup golden raisins
1 can (8¾ ounces) sliced peaches in heavy syrup, drained, chopped and syrup reserved
1 tablespoon cornstarch
¼ cup orange juice
1 can (8¼ ounces) crushed pineapple in syrup, undrained
1 tablespoon grated orange peel
1 clove garlic, minced
½ teaspoon red pepper flakes
½ teaspoon grated fresh ginger

Merry Main Dishes

Rack of Lamb with Orange Carrot Stuffing

2 **American lamb racks,
8 ribs each, French cut**
½ **cup chicken broth**
2 **carrots, shredded**
1 **zucchini, shredded**
1 **onion, chopped**
1 **rib celery, chopped**
3 **cups dried whole wheat
or multigrain bread
cubes**
1 **medium orange, peeled,
seeded and chopped**
¼ **cup chopped fresh parsley**
2 **teaspoons finely grated
orange peel**
½ **teaspoon ground nutmeg**
½ **teaspoon dried sage
leaves**
½ **teaspoon dried thyme
leaves**
½ **teaspoon dried mint
leaves**
2 **tablespoons orange juice
concentrate**

Trim lamb racks well. In medium saucepan, heat chicken broth. Add carrots, zucchini, onion and celery; simmer, covered, about 10 minutes, stirring occasionally.

Stir bread cubes, orange, parsley, orange peel and spices into vegetable mixture. If too dry, add extra broth. *Do not overmix.*

On broiler pan grid, press 2 lamb racks together so bones interlock at top and stuffing is in center. Tie if necessary. Brush each rack with orange juice concentrate.

Roast in preheated 375°F oven for 30 minutes or until internal temperature reaches 145° to 150°F. Turn oven off and let racks rest 5 minutes in oven.

Makes 8 servings

Favorite recipe from **American Lamb Council**

Merry Main Dishes

Roast Turkey with Herb Stuffing

1. Preheat oven to 350°F. Place breadstick cubes on nonstick baking sheet. Bake 20 minutes to dry.

2. Remove giblets from turkey. Melt butter in large nonstick skillet. Add mushrooms, onion and celery. Cook and stir 5 minutes or until onion is soft and golden; remove from heat. Add parsley, tarragon, thyme, pepper and bread cubes; stir until blended. Gently mix chicken broth into bread cube mixture. Fill turkey cavities with stuffing.

3. Spray roasting pan with nonstick cooking spray. Place turkey, breast side up, in roasting pan. Bake at 350°F 3 hours or until meat thermometer inserted into thigh registers 180°F and juices run clear.

4. Transfer turkey to serving platter. Cover loosely with foil; let stand 20 minutes. Slice turkey and serve with herb stuffing.   *Makes 10 servings*

4 cups cubed fresh herb- or garlic-flavored breadsticks
1 turkey (8 to 10 pounds)
1 tablespoon butter
1½ cups sliced mushrooms
1 cup chopped onion
⅔ cup chopped celery
¼ cup chopped fresh parsley
1 to 2 tablespoons chopped fresh tarragon
1 tablespoon chopped fresh thyme
¼ teaspoon black pepper
¼ cup reduced-sodium chicken broth

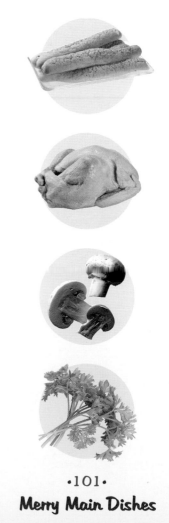

Cornish Hens with Citrus Chutney Glaze

Grated peel and juice of
1 SUNKIST® orange
Grated peel and juice of
1 SUNKIST® lemon
¼ cup bottled mango
chutney
1 tablespoon margarine or
butter
4 Rock Cornish game hens
(1¼ to 1½ pounds
each), thawed if frozen
(giblets and necks
removed)

For glaze, in small saucepan combine citrus peels and juices, chutney and margarine. Simmer 5 minutes to blend flavors, breaking up any mango pieces with back of spoon. Tie legs of each hen together with string and turn wing tips under back of each hen. Brush hens lightly with glaze and arrange, breast side up, in shallow baking pan lined with aluminum foil. Bake at 350°F for 1 hour to 1 hour and 15 minutes or until hens are tender, brushing occasionally with remaining glaze. (Cover legs and wings with small pieces of foil if they start to become too brown.) Remove string before serving.

Makes 4 servings

Merry Main Dishes

Beef Pot Roast

1. Heat Dutch oven over medium-high heat. Brown roast evenly on all sides.

2. Pour broth into Dutch oven; bring to a boil over high heat. Add garlic and herbes de Provence. Cover and reduce heat; simmer 1½ hours.

3. Add turnips, brussels sprouts, carrots and onions to Dutch oven. Cover; cook 25 to 30 minutes or until vegetables are tender. Remove meat and vegetables; arrange on serving platter. Cover with foil to keep warm.

4. Strain broth; return to Dutch oven. Stir water into cornstarch until smooth. Stir cornstarch mixture into broth. Bring to a boil over medium-high heat; cook and stir 1 minute or until thick and bubbly. Serve immediately with pot roast and vegetables. *Makes 8 servings*

1 beef eye of round roast (about 2½ pounds)
1 can (about 14 ounces) fat-free reduced-sodium beef broth
2 cloves garlic
1 teaspoon herbes de Provence *or* ¼ teaspoon *each* dried rosemary, thyme, sage and savory
4 small turnips, peeled and cut into wedges
10 ounces fresh brussels sprouts, trimmed
8 ounces baby carrots
4 ounces pearl onions, skins removed
1 tablespoon water
2 teaspoons cornstarch

Merry Main Dishes

Dazzling Desserts

Pumpkin Cheesecake with Gingersnap-Pecan Crust

Crust

1¼ cups gingersnap cookie crumbs (about 24 cookies)

⅓ cup pecans, very finely chopped

¼ cup sugar

¼ cup (½ stick) butter, melted

Filling

3 packages (8 ounces each) cream cheese, softened

1 cup packed light brown sugar

1 teaspoon cinnamon

½ teaspoon ground ginger

¼ teaspoon ground nutmeg

2 eggs

2 egg yolks

1 cup solid-pack pumpkin

1. Preheat oven to 350°F. For crust, combine cookie crumbs, pecans, sugar and butter in medium bowl; mix well. Press crumb mixture evenly on bottom of ungreased 9-inch springform pan. Bake 8 to 10 minutes or until golden brown.

2. Meanwhile for filling, beat cream cheese in large bowl with electric mixer at medium speed until fluffy. Add brown sugar, cinnamon, ginger and nutmeg; beat until well blended. Beat in eggs and egg yolks, one at a time, beating well after each addition. Add pumpkin; beat until well blended.

3. Pour mixture into baked crust. Bake 1 hour or until edges are set but center is still moist. Turn off oven; let cheesecake stand in oven with door ajar 30 minutes. Transfer to wire rack. To prevent cracking, loosen edge of cake from rim of pan with thin metal spatula; cool completely.

4. Cover; refrigerate at least 24 hours or up to 48 hours before serving.

Makes 10 to 12 servings

Tip: To help prevent the cheesecake from cracking while baking, place a pan of water in the oven to help create moist heat.

Grandma's® Gingerbread

½ cup shortening or butter
½ cup sugar
1 cup GRANDMA'S®
   Molasses
2 eggs
2½ cups all-purpose flour
2 teaspoons baking powder
2 teaspoons cinnamon
1 teaspoon salt
1 teaspoon ground ginger
½ teaspoon baking soda
½ teaspoon ground cloves
1 cup hot water

Heat oven to 350°F. In medium bowl, blend shortening with sugar. Add molasses and eggs; beat well. Sift dry ingredients; add alternately with water to molasses mixture. Bake in greased 9-inch square pan about 50 minutes.

Makes 8 servings

Hint: Just before serving, dust top of cake lightly with powdered sugar, if desired.

Holiday Bread Pudding

PREHEAT oven to 350°F. Grease 12×8-inch baking dish.

COMBINE bread and cranberries in large bowl. Combine evaporated milk, eggs, butter, sugar, vanilla extract, cinnamon and nutmeg in medium bowl. Pour egg mixture over bread mixture; mix well. Pour mixture into prepared baking dish. Let stand for 10 minutes.

BAKE for 35 to 45 minutes or until knife inserted in center comes out clean. Top with caramel sauce. Garnish as desired.   *Makes 8 servings*

16 slices bread, cubed
1 cup dried cranberries or raisins
2 cans (12 fluid ounces *each*) NESTLÉ® CARNATION® Evaporated Milk
4 large eggs, lightly beaten
4 tablespoons butter, melted
¾ cup packed brown sugar
1 tablespoon vanilla extract
1 teaspoon ground cinnamon
½ teaspoon ground nutmeg Caramel sauce (optional)

Dazzling Desserts

Cranberry Swirl Pumpkin Cheesecake

2 packages (8 ounces each) cream cheese, softened
½ cup sugar
1 teaspoon vanilla
2 eggs
1 can (15 ounces) solid-pack pumpkin
1 teaspoon ground cinnamon
½ teaspoon ground nutmeg
½ teaspoon ground ginger
½ teaspoon ground cloves
Pinch of salt
1 (9-inch) graham cracker crust
1 (10-ounce) tub frozen cranberry-orange sauce, thawed and puréed in food processor

1. Preheat oven to 350°F. Beat cream cheese, sugar and vanilla in large bowl with electric mixer at medium speed until smooth and well blended. Add eggs, one at a time, beating well after each addition. Add pumpkin, spices and salt; beat until well blended.

2. Spread ¾ cup pumpkin mixture evenly in crust. Pour about ⅓ cup cranberry sauce over pumpkin mixture. Top with remaining pumpkin mixture and remaining cranberry sauce. Swirl cranberry sauce into pumpkin mixture with knife, being careful not to scrape crust.

3. Bake 50 to 60 minutes. (Cheesecake will not be completely set in center.) Cool completely on wire rack. Refrigerate at least 2 hours or overnight.

Makes 8 servings

Variation: Add ¼ teaspoon salt and additional 1 teaspoon ground cinnamon to pumpkin mixture. Fold cranberry sauce into pumpkin mixture instead of swirling. Pour into crust; bake as directed above.

Upside-Down Pear Tart

1. Heat sugar in heavy 10-inch skillet with oven-safe handle over medium heat until syrupy and light brown in color. Remove from heat. Add butter and lemon peel; stir until butter melts.

2. Arrange pears in two layers over hot sugar mixture in skillet. Fill open spaces with pear slices; sprinkle with lemon juice. Roll pastry to 10-inch round and place over pears.

3. Bake at 425°F 25 to 30 minutes or until pastry is golden brown. Cool, in pan, 30 minutes. If there seems to be too much sauce in pan, pour excess sauce into 1-pint container and reserve to serve over tart. Invert tart onto shallow serving dish. Serve warm with yogurt.   *Makes 6 to 8 servings*

Favorite recipe from **Pear Bureau Northwest**

½ cup sugar
2 tablespoons butter or margarine
2 teaspoons grated lemon peel
5 medium (2½ to 3 pounds) firm USA winter pears, peeled, cored and cut into eighths
1 tablespoon lemon juice
Pastry for 9-inch single crust pie
Vanilla yogurt

Dazzling Desserts

Orange Pecan Pie

3 eggs
½ cup GRANDMA'S® Molasses
½ cup light corn syrup
¼ cup orange juice
1 teaspoon grated orange peel
1 teaspoon vanilla
1½ cups whole pecan halves
1 (9-inch) unbaked pie shell
Whipped cream (optional)

Heat oven to 350°F. In large bowl, beat eggs. Add molasses, corn syrup, orange juice, orange peel and vanilla; beat until well blended. Stir in pecans. Pour into unbaked pie shell. Bake 30 to 45 minutes or until filling sets. Cool on wire rack. Garnish as desired. Serve with whipped cream, if desired.

Makes 8 servings

Cran-Raspberry Hazelnut Trifle

1. Combine dairy creamer and pudding mix in medium bowl; beat with wire whisk 1 to 2 minutes or until thickened.

2. Cut pound cake into ¾-inch cubes. Combine pie filling and cranberry sauce in medium bowl; blend well.

3. Layer one third of cake cubes, one third of fruit sauce and one third of pudding mixture in 1½- to 2-quart straight-sided glass serving bowl. Repeat layers twice. Cover; refrigerate until serving time. Garnish with whipped topping, fresh raspberries and fresh mint sprigs.   *Makes 8 servings*

2 cups hazelnut-flavored liquid dairy creamer

1 package (3.4 ounces) instant vanilla pudding and pie filling mix

1 package (about 11 ounces) frozen pound cake, thawed

1 can (21 ounces) raspberry pie filling

1 can (16 ounces) whole berry cranberry sauce

Whipped topping, fresh raspberries and fresh mint sprigs (optional)

Fireside Steamed Pudding

1½ cups plain dry bread crumbs
1 cup sugar, divided
2 tablespoons all-purpose flour
½ teaspoon baking powder
⅛ teaspoon salt
6 eggs, separated
1 can (21 ounces) cherry pie filling, divided
2 tablespoons butter or margarine, melted
½ teaspoon almond extract
¼ teaspoon red food color
1 cup HERSHEY'S MINI CHIPS™ Semi-Sweet Chocolate Chips
Cherry Whipped Cream (recipe follows)

1. Thoroughly grease 8-cup tube mold or heat-proof bowl.

2. Stir together bread crumbs, ¾ cup sugar, flour, baking powder and salt in large bowl. Stir together egg yolks, 1½ cups cherry pie filling, butter, almond extract and food color in medium bowl; add to crumb mixture, stirring gently until well blended.

3. Beat egg whites in another large bowl until foamy; gradually add remaining ¼ cup sugar, beating until stiff peaks form. Fold about ⅓ beaten whites into cherry mixture, blending thoroughly. Fold in remaining egg whites; gently fold in small chocolate chips. Pour batter into prepared tube mold. (If mold is open at top, cover opening with foil; grease top of foil.) Cover mold with wax paper and foil; tie securely with string.

4. Place rack in large kettle; pour water into kettle to top of rack. Heat water to boiling; place mold on rack. Cover kettle; steam over simmering water about 1½ hours or until wooden pick inserted comes out clean. (Additional water may be needed during steaming.) Remove from heat; cool in pan 5 minutes. Remove cover; unmold onto serving plate. Serve warm with Cherry Whipped Cream. *Makes 12 to 14 servings*

Cherry Whipped Cream: Beat 1 cup (½ pint) cold whipping cream with ¼ cup powdered sugar in medium bowl until stiff; fold in pie filling remaining from pudding (about ½ cup) and ½ teaspoon almond extract.

Dazzling Desserts

Bourbon-Laced Sweet Potato Pie

1. Preheat oven to 350°F. Place sweet potatoes in saucepan; cover with water. Simmer about 20 minutes or until very tender. Drain well in colander; transfer to large bowl. Add butter; beat until potatoes are smooth. Add brown sugar, cinnamon and salt; beat until well blended. Beat in eggs one at a time. Beat in cream and bourbon.

2. Line ungreased 9-inch pie plate (not deep-dish) with pastry; flute edges. Pour sweet potato mixture into crust. Bake 50 minutes or until knife inserted into center comes out clean. Transfer to wire rack; cool at least 1 hour before serving. Serve warm or at room temperature with whipped cream.

Makes 8 servings

Tip: Pie may be cooled completely, covered and chilled up to 24 hours before serving. Let stand at room temperature at least 30 minute before serving.

1 pound (2 medium) sweet potatoes, peeled, cut into 1-inch chunks
2 tablespoons butter
¾ cup packed brown sugar
1 teaspoon ground cinnamon
¼ teaspoon salt
2 eggs
¾ cup whipping cream
¼ cup bourbon or whiskey
Pastry for 9-inch pie (or half of 15-ounce package refrigerated pastry crusts)
Sweetened whipped cream

Easy Fudge Pots de Crème

1 package (4-serving size) chocolate cook & serve pudding and pie filling mix*
2 cups half-and-half or whole milk
1 cup HERSHEY'S Semi-Sweet Chocolate Chips
Sweetened whipped cream
HERSHEY'S Cocoa (optional)

*Do not use instant pudding mix.

1. Stir together pudding mix and half-and-half in medium saucepan. Cook over medium heat, stirring constantly, until mixture comes to a full boil. Remove from heat.

2. Add chocolate chips; stir until chips are melted and mixture is smooth.

3. Spoon into demitasse cups or small dessert dishes. Press plastic wrap directly onto surface. Refrigerate several hours or until chilled. Garnish with whipped cream; sift cocoa over top, if desired. *Makes 8 servings*

Dazzling Desserts

Apple Cranberry Crisp

1. Preheat oven to 350°F. Grease shallow 2-quart baking dish.

2. Combine ½ cup brown sugar, cornstarch, cinnamon, ginger and nutmeg in large bowl. Add apples, cranberries and orange peel; toss to mix well. Spoon into prepared dish.

3. Combine baking mix, oats, nuts, remaining ½ cup brown sugar and salt in medium bowl. Cut in butter with pastry blender or 2 knives until mixture resembles coarse crumbs. Sprinkle over apple mixture.

4. Bake 50 minutes or until apples are tender. Serve warm with ice cream.

Makes 6 to 8 servings

1 cup brown sugar, divided
1 tablespoon cornstarch
1 teaspoon ground cinnamon
½ teaspoon ground ginger
¼ teaspoon ground nutmeg
5 to 6 cups cubed peeled tart apples
1 cup fresh or frozen cranberries *or* ½ cup dried cranberries
1 teaspoon freshly grated orange peel
½ cup buttermilk baking mix
½ cup uncooked oats
½ cup coarsely chopped walnuts
¼ teaspoon salt
¼ cup (½ stick) butter
Ice cream (optional)

Libby's® Famous Pumpkin Pie

MIX sugar, cinnamon, salt, ginger and cloves in small bowl. Beat eggs in large bowl. Stir in pumpkin and sugar-spice mixture. Gradually stir in evaporated milk.

POUR into pie shell.

BAKE in preheated 425°F. oven for 15 minutes. Reduce temperature to 350°F.; bake for 40 to 50 minutes or until knife inserted near center comes out clean. Cool on wire rack for 2 hours. Serve immediately or refrigerate. Top with whipped cream before serving. *Makes 8 servings*

Note: Do not freeze, as this will cause the crust to separate from the filling.

Tip: 1¾ teaspoons pumpkin pie spice may be substituted for the cinnamon, ginger and cloves; however, the taste will be slightly different.

For 2 shallow pies: Substitute two 9-inch (2-cup volume) pie shells. Bake in preheated 425°F. oven for 15 minutes. Reduce temperature to 350°F.; bake for 20 to 30 minutes or until pies test done.

¾ cup granulated sugar
1 teaspoon ground cinnamon
½ teaspoon salt
½ teaspoon ground ginger
¼ teaspoon ground cloves
2 large eggs
1 can (15 ounces) LIBBY'S® 100% Pure Pumpkin
1 can (12 fluid ounces) NESTLÉ® CARNATION® Evaporated Milk
1 *unbaked* 9-inch (4-cup volume) deep-dish pie shell
Whipped cream

Dazzling Desserts

Traditional Fruit Cake

1. Preheat oven to 300°F. Line 9×5-inch loaf pan with greased waxed paper.

2. Combine walnuts and fruit in large bowl; set aside.

3. Combine flour, sugar, baking powder and salt in medium bowl. Sift over walnut mixture; toss gently until walnut mixture is well coated.

4. Blend in eggs, rum, orange peel and vanilla. Spread in prepared pan.

5. Bake 1 hour 45 minutes or until golden brown. Cool completely in pan on wire rack.

Makes 1 (9×5-inch) loaf

3 cups walnut halves
1 package (8 ounces) candied cherries
1 package (8 ounces) chopped dates
1 package (4 ounces) candied pineapple
¾ cup sifted all-purpose flour
¾ cup sugar
½ teaspoon baking powder
½ teaspoon salt
3 eggs, lightly beaten
3 tablespoons dark rum or rum extract
1 tablespoon freshly grated orange peel
1 teaspoon vanilla

Dark Rum

Easy Egg Nog Pound Cake

1 (18.25-ounce) package
   yellow cake mix
1 (4-serving size) package
   instant vanilla pudding
   and pie filling mix
¾ cup BORDEN® Egg Nog
¾ cup vegetable oil
 4 eggs
½ teaspoon ground nutmeg
   Powdered sugar
   (optional)

1. Preheat oven to 350°F. In large bowl, combine cake mix, pudding mix, Borden® Egg Nog and oil; beat at low speed of electric mixer until moistened. Add eggs and nutmeg; beat at medium-high speed 4 minutes.

2. Pour into greased and floured 10-inch fluted or tube pan.

3. Bake 40 to 45 minutes or until wooden pick inserted near center comes out clean.

4. Cool 10 minutes; remove from pan. Cool completely. Sprinkle with powdered sugar (optional).   *Makes 1 (10-inch) cake*

Prep Time: *10 minutes*
Bake Time: *40 to 45 minutes*

Dazzling Desserts

Cherry-Glazed Chocolate Torte

1. Heat oven to 350°F. Grease bottom of 9-inch springform pan.

2. Stir together butter, sugar and vanilla in large bowl. Add eggs; using spoon, beat well. Stir together flour, cocoa, baking powder and salt; gradually add to egg mixture, beating until well blended. Spread batter in prepared pan.

3. Bake 25 to 30 minutes or until cake is set. (Cake will be fudgey and will not test done.) Remove from oven; cool completely in pan on wire rack.

4. Beat cream cheese and powdered sugar in medium bowl until well blended; gradually fold in whipped topping, blending well. Spread over top of cake. Spread 1 cup cherry pie filling over cream layer; refrigerate several hours. With knife, loosen cake from side of pan; remove side of pan. Cut into wedges; garnish with remaining pie filling. Cover; refrigerate leftover dessert.

Makes 10 to 12 servings

½ cup (1 stick) butter or margarine, melted
1 cup granulated sugar
1 teaspoon vanilla extract
2 eggs
½ cup all-purpose flour
⅓ cup HERSHEY'S Cocoa
¼ teaspoon baking powder
¼ teaspoon salt
1 package (8 ounces) cream cheese, softened
1 cup powdered sugar
1 cup frozen non-dairy whipped topping, thawed
1 can (21 ounces) cherry pie filling, divided

Dazzling Desserts

Chocolate Marble & Praline Cheesecake

Crust
1½ vanilla wafer crumbs
¼ cup powdered sugar
¼ cup (½ stick) butter, melted
½ cup finely chopped toasted pecans*

Filling
1¼ cups packed brown sugar
2 tablespoons all-purpose flour
3 packages (8 ounces each) cream cheese, softened
3 eggs, lightly beaten
1½ teaspoons vanilla
1 square (1 ounce) unsweetened chocolate, melted
20 to 25 pecan halves (½ cup)
Caramel ice cream topping

To toast nuts, place on baking sheet. Bake at 350°F 5 to 7 minutes or until lightly browned.

1. Preheat oven to 350°F.

2. For crust, combine crumbs, powdered sugar, butter and pecans in large bowl; mix well. Press mixture onto bottom and up side of ungreased 9-inch springform pan. Bake 10 to 15 minutes or until lightly browned. Transfer to wire rack.

3. For filling, combine brown sugar and flour in small bowl; mix well. Beat cream cheese in large bowl with electric mixer at low speed until fluffy; gradually add brown sugar mixture. Add eggs and vanilla; beat just until blended. Remove 1 cup batter to small bowl; stir in chocolate. Pour remaining plain batter over warm crust.

4. Drop spoonfuls of chocolate batter over plain batter. Run knife through batters to marbleize. Arrange pecan halves around edge. Bake 45 to 55 minutes or until set. Loosen cake from side of pan. Cool completely on wire rack. Refrigerate 2 hours or until ready to serve.

5. To serve, remove side of pan. Glaze top of cheesecake with caramel topping.

Makes 12 to 16 servings

Chocolate & Creamy Orange Mousse

1. Melt butter in heavy saucepan over low heat; add cocoa, then $^2/_3$ cup sweetened condensed milk, stirring until smooth and slightly thickened. Pour mixture into medium bowl; cool to room temperature. Beat in 1 tablespoon orange juice and 1 teaspoon orange peel.

2. Beat whipping cream in large bowl until stiff. Fold half of whipped cream into chocolate mixture. In second medium bowl, stir together remaining sweetened condensed milk, remaining 1 tablespoon orange juice and 1 teaspoon orange peel. Fold in remaining whipped cream.

3. Spoon equal portions of chocolate mixture into 8 dessert dishes, making a depression in center of each. Spoon creamy orange mixture into center of each. Refrigerate until well chilled. Garnish as desired. Cover; refrigerate leftover dessert. *Makes 8 servings*

¼ cup (½ stick) butter or margarine
¼ cup HERSHEY'S Cocoa
1 can (14 ounces) sweetened condensed milk (not evaporated milk), divided
2 tablespoons orange juice plus 2 teaspoons freshly grated orange peel or 2 tablespoons orange-flavored liqueur, divided
2 cups (1 pint) cold whipping cream

Dazzling Desserts

Mini Kisses Pumpkin Mousse Cups

1¾ cups (10-ounce package) HERSHEY'S MINI KISSES® Brand Milk Chocolates, divided
24 marshmallows
½ cup milk
½ cup canned pumpkin
1 teaspoon vanilla extract
1 teaspoon pumpkin pie spice
⅓ cup powdered sugar
1 cup (½ pint) cold whipping cream

1. Line 10 muffin cups (2½ inches in diameter) with paper bake cups. Reserve ½ cup chocolates pieces. Place remaining 1¼ cups chocolates in small microwave-safe bowl; microwave at HIGH (100%) 1 minute or until melted when stirred. Mixture should be thick.

2. Very thickly coat inside pleated surfaces and bottoms of bake cups with melted chocolate using soft pastry brush. Refrigerate 10 minutes; recoat any thin spots with melted chocolate.* Refrigerate until firm, about 2 hours. Gently peel off paper; refrigerate until ready to fill.

3. Place marshmallows, milk, and pumpkin in medium microwave-safe bowl. Microwave at HIGH 1 minute; stir. Microwave additional 30 seconds at a time, stirring after each heating, until mixture is melted and smooth. Stir in vanilla and pumpkin pie spice. Cool completely.

4. Beat powdered sugar and whipping cream until stiff; fold into pumpkin mixture. Fill cups with pumpkin mousse; garnish with whipped cream and reserved chocolates pieces. Cover; refrigerate 2 hours or until firm.

Makes 10 servings

If reheating is needed, microwave chocolate at HIGH 15 seconds; stir.

Dazzling Desserts

Poached Pears in Cranberry Syrup

1. In heavy 4-quart saucepot combine cranberry juice, corn syrup, ginger and cinnamon sticks; bring to a boil over medium-high heat.

2. Peel pears, leaving stems attached. Add to cranberry liquid; cover. Reduce heat and simmer 15 to 20 minutes or until pears are tender. With slotted spoon transfer pears to shallow serving dish.

3. Remove ginger slices and cinnamon sticks. Discard all but 2 cups syrup in saucepot. Bring to a boil; boil 10 to 12 minutes or until syrup thickens slightly. Spoon sauce over pears.   *Makes 8 servings*

Prep Time: *40 minutes*

1 quart (4 cups) cranberry juice
1 cup KARO® Light Corn Syrup
8 slices (¼ inch thick) unpeeled fresh ginger
2 cinnamon sticks (2 to 3 inches)
8 slightly underripe pears

Pumpkin Carrot Cake

2 cups all-purpose flour
2 teaspoons baking soda
2 teaspoons ground
 cinnamon
½ teaspoon salt
¾ cup milk
1½ teaspoons lemon juice
3 large eggs
1¼ cups LIBBY'S® 100%
 Pure Pumpkin
1½ cups granulated sugar
½ cup packed brown sugar
½ cup vegetable oil
1 can (8 ounces) crushed
 pineapple, drained
1 cup (about 3 medium)
 grated carrots
1 cup flaked coconut
1¼ cups chopped nuts,
 divided
 Cream Cheese Frosting
 (recipe follows)

PREHEAT oven to 350°F. Grease two 9-inch round baking pans.

COMBINE flour, baking soda, cinnamon and salt in small bowl. Combine milk and lemon juice in liquid measuring cup (mixture will appear curdled).

BEAT eggs, pumpkin, granulated sugar, brown sugar, oil, pineapple, carrots and milk mixture in large mixer bowl; mix well. Gradually add flour mixture; beat until combined. Stir in coconut and *1 cup* nuts. Pour into prepared baking pans.

BAKE for 30 to 35 minutes or until wooden pick inserted in center comes out clean. Cool in pans for 15 minutes. Remove to wire racks to cool completely.

FROST between layers, on side and top of cake with Cream Cheese Frosting. Garnish with *remaining* nuts. Store in refrigerator. *Makes 12 servings*

Cream Cheese Frosting: **COMBINE** 11 ounces softened cream cheese, ⅓ cup softened butter and 3½ cups sifted powdered sugar in large mixer bowl until fluffy. Add 1 teaspoon vanilla extract, 2 teaspoons orange juice and 1 teaspoon grated orange peel; beat until combined.

*Crushed
Pineapple*

Dazzling Desserts

Cranberry-Orange Rice Pudding

1. Combine rice and orange peel in 3-quart saucepan; cook rice according to package directions.

2. Meanwhile, combine cranberries and orange juice in saucepan; bring to a simmer over medium heat. Simmer 7 minutes or until juice is absorbed. Set aside.

3. Add milk, evaporated milk, sugar and salt to cooked rice. Cook and stir over medium-low heat about 40 minutes or until slightly thickened.

4. Stir cranberries into rice mixture. Cool to room temperature. Refrigerate until serving time.   *Makes 8 servings*

1 cup long-grain rice*
1 tablespoon freshly grated orange peel
1½ cups dried cranberries, coarsely chopped
½ cup orange juice
1 quart (4 cups) milk
1 can (12 ounces) evaporated milk
⅔ cup sugar
⅛ teaspoon salt

*1½ cups parboiled quick-cooking rice or 3 cups cooked rice can be substituted.

Dazzling Desserts

Chocolate Truffle Torte

1½ cups milk

1 package (12 ounces) semisweet chocolate chips

6 squares (1 ounce each) unsweetened baking chocolate, chopped

1 cup packed brown sugar

1 container (8 ounces) pasteurized cholesterol-free egg substitute

2 teaspoons vanilla

1. Heat milk in medium saucepan over medium-low heat just until bubbles appear around edge of saucepan.

2. Combine chocolate chips, chopped chocolate and brown sugar in blender. Pour hot milk into blender; carefully blend until smooth. With blender still running, add egg substitute and vanilla.

3. Pour chocolate mixture into 9-inch springform pan. Cover and chill at least 6 hours or overnight. Garnish as desired. *Makes 10 to 12 servings*

Pumpkin Dutch Apple Pie

PREHEAT oven to 375°F.

For Apple Layer

COMBINE apples with sugar, flour, lemon juice and cinnamon in medium bowl; pour into pie shell.

For Pumpkin Layer

COMBINE pumpkin, evaporated milk, sugar, eggs, butter, cinnamon, salt and nutmeg in medium bowl; pour over apple mixture.

BAKE for 30 minutes. Remove from oven; sprinkle with Crumb Topping. Return to oven; bake for 20 minutes or until custard is set. Cool completely on wire rack. *Makes 8 servings*

Crumb Topping: **COMBINE** ½ cup all-purpose flour, ⅓ cup chopped walnuts and 5 tablespoons granulated sugar in medium bowl. Cut in 3 tablespoons butter with pastry blender or two knives until mixtures resembles coarse crumbs.

Apple Layer
- 2 cups (about 2 medium) peeled, cored, thinly sliced green apples
- ¼ cup granulated sugar
- 2 teaspoons all-purpose flour
- 1 teaspoon lemon juice
- ¼ teaspoon cinnamon
- 1 *unbaked* 9-inch (4-cup volume) deep-dish pie shell with fluted edge

Pumpkin Layer
- 1½ cups LIBBY'S® 100% Pure Pumpkin
- 1 cup NESTLÉ® CARNATION® Evaporated Milk
- ½ cup granulated sugar
- 2 large eggs, lightly beaten
- 2 tablespoons butter or margarine, melted
- ¾ teaspoon cinnamon
- ¼ teaspoon salt
- ⅛ teaspoon ground nutmeg
  Crumb Topping (recipe follows)

White Chocolate Cranberry Tart

1 refrigerated pie crust
1 cup sugar
2 eggs
¼ cup (½ stick) butter,
   melted
2 teaspoons vanilla
½ cup all-purpose flour
6 squares (1 ounce each)
   white chocolate,
   chopped
½ cup chopped macadamia
   nuts, lightly toasted*
½ cup dried cranberries,
   coarsely chopped

*Toast chopped macadamia nuts in
hot skillet over medium heat about
3 minutes or until fragrant.

1. Preheat oven to 350°F. Place pie crust in 9-inch tart pan with removable bottom or pie pan. (Refrigerate or freeze other crust for another use.)

2. Combine sugar, eggs, butter and vanilla in large bowl; mix well. Stir in flour until well blended. Add white chocolate, nuts and cranberries.

3. Pour filling into unbaked crust. Bake 50 to 55 minutes or until top of tart is crusty and deep golden brown, and knife inserted into center comes out clean.

4. Cool completely on wire rack. *Makes 8 servings*

Hint: Top each serving with a dollop of whipped cream flavored with ground cinnamon, a favorite liqueur and grated orange peel.

Pie Crusts

Pumpkin Pie Crunch

1. Preheat oven to 350°F. Grease bottom only of 13×9×2-inch baking pan.

2. Combine pumpkin, evaporated milk, eggs, sugar, pumpkin pie spice and salt in large bowl. Pour into prepared pan. Sprinkle dry cake mix evenly over pumpkin mixture. Top with pecans. Drizzle with melted butter. Bake at 350°F for 50 to 55 minutes or until golden. Cool completely. Serve with whipped topping. Refrigerate leftovers. *Makes 16 to 20 servings*

Tip: For a richer flavor, try using Duncan Hines® Moist Deluxe® Butter Recipe Golden Cake Mix.

1 can (16 ounces) solid pack pumpkin
1 can (12 ounces) evaporated milk
3 eggs
1½ cups sugar
4 teaspoons pumpkin pie spice
½ teaspoon salt
1 package DUNCAN HINES® Moist Deluxe® Classic Yellow Cake Mix
1 cup chopped pecans
1 cup butter or margarine, melted
Whipped topping

Sugarplum Delights

Peanut Butter Truffles

2 cups (11½ ounces) milk chocolate chips
½ cup whipping cream
2 tablespoons butter
½ cup creamy peanut butter
¾ cup finely chopped peanuts

1. Combine chocolate chips, whipping cream and butter in heavy, medium saucepan; melt over low heat, stirring occasionally. Add peanut butter; stir until blended. Pour into pie pan. Refrigerate about 1 hour or until mixture is fudgy but soft, stirring occasionally.

2. Shape mixture by tablespoonfuls into 1¼-inch balls; place on waxed paper.

3. Place peanuts in shallow bowl. Roll balls in peanuts; place in petit four or paper candy cups. (If peanuts won't stick because truffle has set, roll truffle between palms until outside is soft.)

4. Truffles can be refrigerated 2 to 3 days or frozen several weeks.

Makes about 36 truffles

Tip: For a pretty contrast, roll some of the truffles in cocoa powder instead of chopped peanuts.

Jingle Bells Chocolate Pretzels

1 cup HERSHEY'S Semi-Sweet Chocolate Chips
1 cup HERSHEY'S Premier White Chips, divided
1 tablespoon plus ½ teaspoon shortening (do not use butter, margarine, spread or oil), divided
About 24 salted or unsalted pretzels (3×2 inches)

1. Cover tray or cookie sheet with wax paper.

2. Place chocolate chips, ⅔ cup white chips and 1 tablespoon shortening in medium microwave-safe bowl. Microwave at HIGH (100%) 1 minute; stir. Microwave at HIGH an additional 1 to 2 minutes, stirring every 30 seconds, until chips are melted when stirred.

3. Using fork, dip each pretzel into chocolate mixture; tap fork on side of bowl to remove excess chocolate. Place coated pretzels on prepared tray.

4. Place remaining ⅓ cup white chips and remaining ½ teaspoon shortening in small microwave-safe bowl. Microwave at HIGH 15 to 30 seconds or until chips are melted when stirred. Using tines of fork, drizzle chip mixture across pretzels. Refrigerate until coating is set. Store in airtight container in cool, dry place.   *Makes about 24 coated pretzels*

White Dipped Pretzels: Cover tray with wax paper. Place 2 cups (12-ounce package) HERSHEY'S Premier White Chips and 2 tablespoons shortening (do not use butter, margarine, spread or oil) in medium microwave-safe bowl. Microwave at HIGH 1 to 2 minutes or until chips are melted when stirred. Dip pretzels as directed above. Place ¼ cup HERSHEY'S Semi-Sweet Chocolate Chips and ¼ teaspoon shortening (do not use butter, margarine, spread or oil) in small microwave-safe bowl. Microwave at HIGH 30 seconds to 1 minute or until chips are melted when stirred. Drizzle melted chocolate across pretzels, using tines of fork. Refrigerate and store as directed above.

Sugarplum Delights

Festive Candy Canes

1. Preheat oven to 350°F. Beat butter and powdered sugar in large bowl with electric mixer at medium speed until light and fluffy. Add egg, peppermint extract and vanilla; beat until well blended. Add flour and salt; beat until well blended. (Dough will be sticky.)

2. Divide dough in half. Tint half of dough with food coloring to desired shade of red. Leave remaining dough plain.

3. For each candy cane, with floured hands, shape heaping teaspoonful dough of each color into 5-inch rope; twist together into candy cane shape. Place 2 inches apart on ungreased cookie sheets.

4. Bake 7 to 8 minutes or just until set and edges are very lightly browned. Cool on cookie sheets 2 minutes. Remove to wire racks to cool completely.

Makes about 2 dozen cookies

¾ cup (1½ sticks) butter, softened
1 cup powdered sugar
1 egg
1 teaspoon peppermint extract
½ teaspoon vanilla
1⅔ cups all-purpose flour
⅛ teaspoon salt
Red food coloring

Chocolate Gingersnaps

¾ cup sugar
1 package (18¼ ounces) chocolate cake mix *without* pudding in the mix
1 tablespoon ground ginger
2 eggs
⅓ cup vegetable oil

1. Preheat oven to 350°F. Spray cookie sheets with nonstick cooking spray. Pour sugar into shallow bowl.

2. Combine cake mix and ginger in large bowl. Add eggs and oil; stir until well blended.

3. Shape tablespoonfuls of dough into 1-inch balls; roll in sugar to coat. Place 2 inches apart on prepared cookie sheets.

4. Bake 10 minutes. Remove to wire racks to cool completely.

Makes about 3 dozen cookies

Sugarplum Delights

Tropical Sugarplums

1. Combine white chocolate chips and corn syrup in large saucepan. Cook and stir over low heat until melted and smooth.

2. Stir in dates, cherries, vanilla and rum extract until well blended. Add gingersnaps; stir until well blended. (Mixture will be stiff.)

3. Shape mixture into ¾-inch balls; roll in coconut. Place in miniature paper candy cups, if desired. Serve immediately or let stand overnight to allow flavors to blend. *Makes about 2 dozen candies*

½ cup white chocolate chips
¼ cup light corn syrup
½ cup chopped dates
¼ cup chopped maraschino cherries, well drained
1 teaspoon vanilla
¼ teaspoon rum extract
1¼ cups crushed gingersnaps
Flaked coconut

Sugarplum Delights

Mincemeat Oatmeal Cookies

½ CRISCO® Butter Flavor Stick or ½ cup CRISCO® Butter Flavor shortening plus additional for greasing
1 cup firmly packed brown sugar
1 egg
1⅓ cups prepared mincemeat
1½ cups PILLSBURY BEST® All-Purpose Flour
1 teaspoon baking soda
½ teaspoon salt
1 cup quick oats (not instant or old-fashioned)
½ cup coarsely chopped walnuts

1. Heat oven to 350°F. Grease baking sheet with shortening. Place sheets of foil on countertop for cooling cookies.

2. Combine ½ cup shortening, sugar and egg in large bowl. Beat at medium speed of electric mixer until well blended. Beat in mincemeat.

3. Combine flour, baking soda and salt. Mix into creamed mixture at low speed until blended. Stir in oats and nuts with spoon.

4. Drop rounded tablespoonfuls of dough 2 inches apart onto prepared baking sheet.

5. Bake at 350°F for 12 minutes or until set and lightly browned around edges. *Do not overbake.* Cool 2 minutes on baking sheet. Remove cookies to foil to cool completely. *Makes about 5 dozen cookies*

Sugarplum Delights

Icicle Ornaments

1. Combine flour and salt in medium bowl. Beat sugar and butter in large bowl at medium speed of electric mixer until fluffy. Beat in white chocolate, egg and vanilla. Gradually add flour mixture. Beat at low speed until well blended. Shape dough into disc. Wrap in plastic wrap and refrigerate 30 minutes or until firm.

2. Preheat oven to 350°F. Grease cookie sheets. Shape heaping tablespoonfuls of dough into 10-inch ropes. Fold each rope in half; twist to make icicle shape, leaving opening at fold and tapering ends. Roll in coarse sugar; sprinkle with colored sugars and decors as desired. Place 1 inch apart on prepared cookie sheets.

3. Bake 8 to 10 minutes or until firm but not browned. Cool on cookie sheets 1 minute. Remove to wire racks; cool completely. Pull ribbon through opening in top of each icicle and tie small knot in ribbon ends, if desired.

Makes about 2½ dozen cookies

2½ cups all-purpose flour
¼ teaspoon salt
1 cup sugar
¾ cup (1½ sticks) unsalted butter, softened
2 squares (1 ounce each) white chocolate, melted
1 egg
1 teaspoon vanilla
Coarse white decorating sugar, colored sugars and decors
Ribbon (optional)

Sugarplum Delights

Chocolate Cherry Bars

1 cup (2 sticks) butter or margarine
¾ cup HERSHEY'S Cocoa or HERSHEY'S Special Dark® Cocoa
2 cups sugar
4 eggs
1½ cups plus ⅓ cup all-purpose flour, divided
⅓ cup chopped almonds
1 can (14 ounces) sweetened condensed milk (not evaporated milk)
½ teaspoon almond extract
1 cup HERSHEY'S MINI KISSES® Brand Milk Chocolates
1 cup chopped maraschino cherries, drained

1. Heat oven to 350°F. Generously grease 13×9×2-inch baking pan.

2. Melt butter in large saucepan over low heat; stir in cocoa until smooth. Remove from heat. Add sugar, 3 eggs, 1½ cups flour and almonds; mix well. Pour into prepared pan. Bake 20 minutes.

3. Meanwhile, whisk together remaining 1 egg, remaining ⅓ cup flour, sweetened condensed milk and almond extract. Pour over baked layer; sprinkle chocolate pieces and cherries over top. Return to oven.

4. Bake additional 20 to 25 minutes or until set and edges are golden brown. Cool completely in pan on wire rack. Refrigerate until cold, 6 hours or overnight. Cut into bars. Cover; refrigerate leftover bars.

Makes about 48 bars

Sugarplum Delights

Berlinerkranser (Little Wreaths)

1. Combine 1 cup shortening and confectioners' sugar in large bowl. Beat at medium speed of electric mixer until well blended. Beat in hard boiled egg yolks, uncooked egg yolks, vanilla and almond extract. Beat in flour, ¼ cup at a time, until well blended. Cover and refrigerate 3 hours.

2. Let dough stand at room temperature until it becomes easy to handle.

3. Heat oven to 350°F. Divide dough into 2 equal portions. Cut each portion into 24 equal pieces. Shape each piece of dough into 5-inch-long rope. Form each rope into wreath or loop 1½ inches apart on ungreased baking sheet, overlapping both ends. Brush each wreath with beaten egg whites; sprinkle with colored sugar crystals. Lightly press cherry piece into top of each wreath.

4. Bake at 350°F for 10 to 12 minutes or until edges are lightly browned. Cool on baking sheets 3 minutes; transfer to cooling racks to cool completely.

Makes 4 dozen cookies

Tip: These wreath-shaped cookies are a Norwegian holiday favorite for the family to bake together.

1 CRISCO® Butter Flavor Stick or 1 cup CRISCO® Butter Flavor shortening
1 cup confectioners' sugar
2 large hard boiled egg yolks, mashed
2 large eggs, separated
1 teaspoon vanilla
1 teaspoon almond extract
2¼ cups PILLSBURY BEST® All-Purpose Flour
Green colored sugar crystals
24 red candied cherries, cut into halves

Sugarplum Delights

Holiday Triple Chocolate Yule Logs

1¾ cups all-purpose flour
¾ cup powdered sugar
¼ cup unsweetened cocoa powder
⅛ teaspoon salt
1 cup (2 sticks) butter, softened
1 teaspoon vanilla
1 cup white chocolate chips
1 cup chocolate sprinkles

1. Combine flour, powdered sugar, cocoa and salt in medium bowl; set aside.

2. Beat butter and vanilla in large bowl with electric mixer at medium-low speed until fluffy. Gradually beat in flour mixture until well blended. Wrap dough in plastic wrap; refrigerate at least 30 minutes.

3. Preheat oven to 350°F. Shape dough into 2-inch logs about ½ inch thick. Place 2 inches apart on ungreased cookie sheets.

4. Bake 12 minutes or until set. Let stand on cookie sheets 2 minutes. Transfer to wire racks; cool completely.

5. Place white chocolate chips in small microwavable bowl. Microwave on HIGH 45 seconds; stir until completely melted. Place chocolate sprinkles in another small bowl. Dip each end of cooled cookies first into white chocolate and then into chocolate sprinkles. Place on wire racks; let stand about 25 minutes or until set.

Makes about 3 dozen cookies

Sugarplum Delights

Coconut Bonbons

1. Line baking sheet with waxed paper; set aside.

2. Combine powdered sugar, coconut, milk, butter and vanilla in medium bowl. Stir until well blended. Shape mixture into 1-inch balls; place on prepared baking sheet. Refrigerate until firm.

3. Combine chocolate chips and shortening in small microwavable bowl. Microwave on HIGH 1 minute; stir. Microwave at 30-second intervals, stirring after each interval, until chocolate is melted and mixture is smooth.

4. Dip bonbons in melted chocolate using toothpick or wooden skewer. Remove excess chocolate by scraping bottom of bonbon across bowl rim; return to prepared baking sheet. Sprinkle with toasted coconut, if desired. Refrigerate until firm. Or drizzle plain bonbons with melted white chocolate, if desired. Store in refrigerator.   *Makes about 3 dozen bonbons*

Gift Idea! Place the bonbons in petit fours or paper candy cups. Arrange some crinkled paper gift basket filler in the bottom of a tin or gift box and nestle the candies in the filler. Or, for party favors or small gifts, place 3 or 4 bonbons in a cellophane bag and tie it with 2 pieces of different colored curling ribbon.

2 cups powdered sugar
1 cup flaked coconut
3 tablespoons evaporated milk
2 tablespoons butter, softened
1 teaspoon vanilla
1 cup (6 ounces) semisweet chocolate chips
1 tablespoon shortening
  Toasted coconut and/or melted white chocolate (optional)

Yuletide Layer Bars

PREHEAT oven to 350°F.

MELT butter in 13×9-inch baking pan in oven; remove from oven. Sprinkle graham cracker crumbs over butter. Stir well; press onto bottom of pan. Sprinkle with nuts, coconut and Shapes & Morsels. Pour sweetened condensed milk evenly over top.

BAKE for 25 to 30 minutes or until light golden brown. Cool completely in pan on wire rack

Makes 2 to 3 dozen bars

½ cup (1 stick) butter
2½ cups graham cracker crumbs
1½ cups chopped nuts
1½ cups flaked coconut
1¾ cups (10-ounce package) NESTLÉ® TOLL HOUSE® Holiday Shapes & Morsels
1 can (14 ounces) NESTLÉ® CARNATION® Sweetened Condensed Milk

Sugarplum Delights

Kringle's Cutouts

1. Cream ⅔ cup shortening, sugar, milk and vanilla in large bowl at medium speed of electric mixer until well blended. Beat in egg. Combine flour, baking powder and salt. Mix into creamed mixture at low speed until blended. Cover; refrigerate several hours or overnight.

2. Heat oven to 375°F. Place sheets of foil on countertop for cooling cookies.

3. Roll dough, half at a time, to ⅛-inch thickness on floured surface. Cut into desired shapes. Place cookies 2 inches apart on ungreased baking sheet. Sprinkle with colored sugar and decors, or leave plain to frost when cool.

4. Bake at 375°F for 7 to 9 minutes. *Do not overbake.* Cool 2 minutes on baking sheet. Remove cookies to foil to cool completely.

Makes about 3 dozen cookies

Hint: Floured pastry cloth and rolling pin cover make rolling out dough easier.

⅔ CRISCO® Butter Flavor Stick or ⅔ cup CRISCO® Butter Flavor shortening
¾ cup sugar
1 tablespoon plus 1 teaspoon milk
1 teaspoon vanilla
1 egg
2 cups PILLSBURY BEST® All-Purpose Flour
1½ teaspoons baking powder
¼ teaspoon salt

Sugarplum Delights

Holiday Peppermint Bark

2 cups (12-ounce package)
NESTLÉ® TOLL
HOUSE® Premier
White Morsels
24 hard peppermint candies,
unwrapped

LINE baking sheet with wax paper.

MICROWAVE morsels in medium, uncovered, microwave-safe bowl on MEDIUM-HIGH (70%) power for 1 minute. STIR. Morsels may retain some of their original shape. If necessary, microwave at additional 10- to 15-second intervals, stirring just until morsels are melted.

PLACE peppermint candies in *heavy-duty* resealable plastic food storage bag. Crush candies using rolling pin or other heavy object. While holding strainer over melted morsels, pour crushed candy into strainer. Shake to release all small candy pieces; reserve larger candy pieces. Stir morsel-peppermint mixture.

SPREAD mixture to desired thickness on prepared baking sheet. Sprinkle with reserved candy pieces; press in lightly. Let stand for about 1 hour or until firm. Break into pieces. Store in airtight container at room temperature.

Makes about 1 pound candy

Sugarplum Delights

Rum Fruitcake Cookies

1. Preheat oven to 375°F. Lightly grease cookie sheets; set aside. Beat sugar and shortening in large bowl until fluffy. Add eggs, orange juice and rum extract; beat 2 minutes.

2. Combine flour, baking powder, baking soda and salt in medium bowl. Add candied fruit, raisins and nuts. Stir into shortening mixture. Drop dough by rounded teaspoonfuls 2 inches apart onto prepared cookie sheets.

3. Bake 10 to 12 minutes or until golden. Let cookies stand on cookie sheets 2 minutes. Remove to wire racks; cool completely.

Makes about 6 dozen cookies

1 cup sugar
¾ cup shortening
3 eggs
⅓ cup orange juice
1 tablespoon rum extract
3 cups all-purpose flour
2 teaspoons baking powder
1 teaspoon baking soda
1 teaspoon salt
2 cups (8 ounces) chopped candied mixed fruit
1 cup raisins
1 cup nuts, coarsely chopped

Golden Kolacky

½ cup (1 stick) butter, softened
4 ounces cream cheese, softened
1 cup all-purpose flour
Fruit preserves

1. Combine butter and cream cheese in large bowl; beat until smooth. Gradually add flour to butter mixture, blending until mixture forms soft dough. Divide dough in half; wrap each half in plastic wrap. Refrigerate about 1 hour or until firm.

2. Preheat oven to 375°F. Roll out dough, half at a time, on floured surface to ⅛-inch thickness. Cut into 2½-inch squares. Spoon 1 teaspoon preserves into center of each square. Bring up two opposite corners to center; pinch together tightly to seal. Fold sealed tip to one side; pinch to seal. Place 1 inch apart on ungreased cookie sheets. Bake 10 to 15 minutes or until lightly browned. Remove to wire racks; cool completely.   *Makes about 2½ dozen cookies*

Sugarplum Delights

Premier Cheesecake Cranberry Bars

PREHEAT oven to 350°F. Grease 13×9-inch baking pan.

COMBINE flour, oats and brown sugar in large bowl. Add butter; mix until crumbly. Stir in morsels. Reserve *2½ cups* morsel mixture for topping. With floured fingers, press *remaining* mixture into prepared pan.

BEAT cream cheese in large mixer bowl until creamy. Add sweetened condensed milk, lemon juice and vanilla extract; mix until smooth. Pour over crust. Combine cranberry sauce and cornstarch in medium bowl. Spoon over cream cheese mixture. Sprinkle *reserved* morsel mixture over cranberry mixture.

BAKE for 35 to 40 minutes or until center is set. Cool completely in pan on wire rack. Cover; refrigerate until serving time (up to 1 day). Cut into bars.

Makes 2½ dozen bars

2 cups all-purpose flour
1½ cups quick or old-
   fashioned oats
¼ cup light brown sugar
1 cup (2 sticks) butter or
   margarine, softened
2 cups (12-ounce package)
   NESTLÉ® TOLL
   HOUSE® Premier
   White Morsels
1 package (8 ounces)
   cream cheese, softened
1 can (14 ounces) NESTLÉ®
   CARNATION®
   Sweetened Condensed
   Milk
¼ cup lemon juice
1 teaspoon vanilla extract
1 can (16 ounces) whole-
   berry cranberry sauce
2 tablespoons cornstarch

Sugarplum Delights

Ornament Brownies

6 squares (1 ounce each)
   semisweet chocolate,
   coarsely chopped
1 tablespoon instant freeze
   dried coffee crystals
1 tablespoon boiling water
¾ cup all-purpose flour
¾ teaspoon ground
   cinnamon
½ teaspoon baking powder
¼ teaspoon salt
½ cup sugar
¼ cup (½ stick) butter,
   softened
2 eggs
   Prepared vanilla frosting
   Assorted food colorings
   Small candy canes,
   assorted candies and
   sprinkles

1. Preheat oven to 350°F. Grease 8-inch square baking pan; set aside. Melt chocolate in small heavy saucepan over low heat, stirring constantly; set aside. Dissolve coffee crystals in boiling water in small cup; set aside.

2. Combine flour, cinnamon, baking powder and salt in small bowl; stir until blended.

3. Beat sugar and butter in large bowl with electric mixer at medium speed until light and fluffy. Beat in eggs, one at a time. Beat in melted chocolate and coffee until well blended. Add flour mixture. Beat at low speed until well blended. Spread batter evenly in prepared pan.

4. Bake 30 to 35 minutes or until center is set. Remove to wire rack; cool completely. Cut into holiday shapes using 2-inch cookie cutters.

5. Tint frosting with food colorings to desired colors. Spread over each brownie shape. Break off top of small candy cane to create loop. Insert in top of brownie. Decorate as desired with assorted candies and sprinkles.

Makes about 8 brownies

Sugarplum Delights

Candy Cane Fudge

1. Line 8-inch baking pan with foil, extending edges over sides of pan.

2. Bring cream and corn syrup to a boil in 2-quart saucepan over medium heat. Boil 1 minute. Remove from heat. Add chocolate chips; stir constantly until chips are melted. Stir in powdered sugar, candy canes and vanilla. Pour into prepared pan. Spread mixture into corners. Cover; refrigerate 2 hours or until firm.

3. Lift fudge out of pan using foil; remove foil. Cut into 1-inch squares. Store in airtight container.   *Makes about 2 pounds fudge or 64 pieces*

½ cup whipping cream
½ cup light corn syrup
3 cups semisweet
   chocolate chips
1½ cups powdered sugar,
   sifted
1 cup candy canes,
   crushed
1½ teaspoons vanilla

Chocolate Mint Truffles

LINE baking sheet with wax paper.

PLACE milk chocolate and semi-sweet morsels in large mixer bowl. Heat cream to a gentle boil in small saucepan; pour over morsels. Let stand for 1 minute; stir until smooth. Stir in peppermint extract. Cover with plastic wrap; refrigerate for 35 to 45 minutes or until slightly thickened. Stir just until color lightens slightly. (*Do not* overmix or truffles will be grainy.)

DROP by rounded teaspoonful onto prepared baking sheet; refrigerate for 10 to 15 minutes. Shape into balls; roll in walnuts or cocoa. Store in airtight container in refrigerator. *Makes about 48 truffles*

Variation: After rolling chocolate mixture into balls, freeze for 30 to 40 minutes. Microwave 1¾ cups (11.5-ounce package) NESTLÉ® TOLL HOUSE® Milk Chocolate Morsels and 3 tablespoons vegetable shortening in medium, uncovered, microwave-safe bowl on MEDIUM-HIGH (70%) power for 1 minute. STIR. Morsels may retain some of their original shape. If necessary, microwave at additional 10- to 15-second intervals, stirring just until morsels are melted. Dip truffles into chocolate mixture; shake off excess. Place on foil-lined baking sheets. Refrigerate for 15 to 20 minutes or until set. Store in airtight container in refrigerator.

1¾ cups (11.5-ounce package) NESTLÉ® TOLL HOUSE® Milk Chocolate Morsels

1 cup (6 ounces) NESTLÉ® TOLL HOUSE® Semi-Sweet Chocolate Morsels

¾ cup heavy whipping cream

1 tablespoon peppermint extract

1½ cups finely chopped walnuts, toasted, or NESTLÉ® TOLL HOUSE® Baking Cocoa

Sugarplum Delights

Christmas Spritz Cookies

1. Preheat oven to 375°F. Combine flour and salt in medium bowl. Combine powdered sugar and butter in large bowl; beat at medium speed of electric mixer until light and fluffy. Beat in egg, almond extract and vanilla. Gradually add flour mixture. Beat until well blended.

2. Divide dough in half. Tint half of dough with green food coloring, if desired. Fit cookie press with desired plate (or change plates for different shapes after first batch). Fill press with dough; press dough 1 inch apart onto ungreased cookie sheets.

3. Bake 10 to 12 minutes or until just set. Remove cookies to wire racks; cool completely.

4. Pipe or drizzle icing onto cooled cookies and decorate with cherries and assorted candies, if desired. Store tightly covered at room temperature or freeze up to 3 months.   *Makes about 5 dozen cookies*

2¼ cups all-purpose flour
¼ teaspoon salt
1¼ cups powdered sugar
1 cup (2 sticks) butter, softened
1 egg
1 teaspoon almond extract
1 teaspoon vanilla
Green food coloring (optional)
Prepared icing (optional)
Candied red and green cherries and assorted decorative candies (optional)

Sugarplum Delights

Creamy Double Decker Fudge

1 cup REESE'S® Peanut
   Butter Chips
1 can (14 ounces)
   sweetened condensed
   milk (not evaporated
   milk), divided
1 teaspoon vanilla extract,
   divided
1 cup HERSHEY'S Semi-
   Sweet Chocolate Chips

1. Line 8-inch square pan with foil.

2. Place peanut butter chips and ⅔ cup sweetened condensed milk in small microwave-safe bowl. Microwave at HIGH (100%) 1 to 1½ minutes, stirring after 1 minute, until chips are melted and mixture is smooth when stirred. Stir in ½ teaspoon vanilla; spread evenly into prepared pan.

3. Place remaining sweetened condensed milk and chocolate chips in another small microwave-safe bowl; repeat above microwave procedure. Stir in remaining ½ teaspoon vanilla; spread evenly over peanut butter layer.

4. Cover; refrigerate until firm. Remove from pan; place on cutting board. Peel off foil. Cut into squares. Store tightly covered in refrigerator.

Makes about 4 dozen pieces or 1½ pounds fudge

Note: For best results, do not double this recipe.

Prep Time: 15 minutes
Cook Time: 3 minutes
Chill Time: 2 hours

Pumpkin White Chocolate Drops

1. Preheat oven to 375°F. Grease cookie sheets.

2. Beat butter and granulated sugar in large bowl with electric mixer at medium speed until light and fluffy. Add pumpkin and eggs; beat until well blended. Add flour, pumpkin pie spice, baking powder and baking soda; beat just until blended. Stir in white chocolate chips.

3. Drop dough by teaspoonfuls about 2 inches apart onto prepared cookie sheets. Bake about 16 minutes or until set and bottoms are browned. Cool 1 minute on cookie sheets. Remove to wire racks to cool completely.

4. Combine frosting and brown sugar in small bowl. Spread on warm cookies.

Makes about 6 dozen cookies

2 cups (4 sticks) butter, softened
2 cups granulated sugar
1 can (about 16 ounces) solid-pack pumpkin
2 eggs
4 cups all-purpose flour
2 teaspoons pumpkin pie spice*
1 teaspoon baking powder
½ teaspoon baking soda
1 package (12 ounces) white chocolate chips
1 container (16 ounces) cream cheese frosting
¼ cup packed brown sugar

*Substitute 1 teaspoon ground cinnamon, ½ teaspoon ground ginger and ¼ teaspoon each ground allspice and ground nutmeg for 2 teaspoons pumpkin pie spice.

Sugarplum Delights

Acknowledgments

The publisher would like to thank the companies and organizations listed below for the use of their recipes and photographs in this publication.

ACH Food Companies, Inc.

American Lamb Council

Birds Eye Foods

Cherry Marketing Institute

Crisco is a registered trademark of The J.M. Smucker Company

Dole Food Company, Inc.

Duncan Hines® and Moist Deluxe® are registered trademarks of Pinnacle Foods Corp.

EAGLE BRAND®

Florida Tomato Committee

Grandma's® is a registered trademark of Mott's, LLP

The Hershey Company

The Hidden Valley® Food Products Company

Hormel Foods, LLC

Lawry's® Foods

McIlhenny Company (TABASCO® brand Pepper Sauce)

National Pork Board

National Turkey Federation

Nestlé USA

Pear Bureau Northwest

Perdue Farms Incorporated

Reckitt Benckiser Inc.

Smucker's® trademark of The J.M. Smucker Company

Reprinted with permission of Sunkist Growers, Inc. All Rights Reserved.

Unilever Foods North America

Veg•All®

Wisconsin Milk Marketing Board

Index

Index

Metric Conversion Chart

VOLUME MEASUREMENTS (dry)

$\frac{1}{8}$ teaspoon = 0.5 mL
$\frac{1}{4}$ teaspoon = 1 mL
$\frac{1}{2}$ teaspoon = 2 mL
$\frac{3}{4}$ teaspoon = 4 mL
1 teaspoon = 5 mL
1 tablespoon = 15 mL
2 tablespoons = 30 mL
$\frac{1}{4}$ cup = 60 mL
$\frac{1}{3}$ cup = 75 mL
$\frac{1}{2}$ cup = 125 mL
$\frac{2}{3}$ cup = 150 mL
$\frac{3}{4}$ cup = 175 mL
1 cup = 250 mL
2 cups = 1 pint = 500 mL
3 cups = 750 mL
4 cups = 1 quart = 1 L

VOLUME MEASUREMENTS (fluid)

1 fluid ounce (2 tablespoons) = 30 mL
4 fluid ounces ($\frac{1}{2}$ cup) = 125 mL
8 fluid ounces (1 cup) = 250 mL
12 fluid ounces (1$\frac{1}{2}$ cups) = 375 mL
16 fluid ounces (2 cups) = 500 mL

WEIGHTS (mass)

$\frac{1}{2}$ ounce = 15 g
1 ounce = 30 g
3 ounces = 90 g
4 ounces = 120 g
8 ounces = 225 g
10 ounces = 285 g
12 ounces = 360 g
16 ounces = 1 pound = 450 g

DIMENSIONS

$\frac{1}{16}$ inch = 2 mm
$\frac{1}{8}$ inch = 3 mm
$\frac{1}{4}$ inch = 6 mm
$\frac{1}{2}$ inch = 1.5 cm
$\frac{3}{4}$ inch = 2 cm
1 inch = 2.5 cm

OVEN TEMPERATURES

250°F = 120°C
275°F = 140°C
300°F = 150°C
325°F = 160°C
350°F = 180°C
375°F = 190°C
400°F = 200°C
425°F = 220°C
450°F = 230°C

BAKING PAN SIZES

Utensil	Size in Inches/Quarts	Metric Volume	Size in Centimeters
Baking or Cake Pan (square or rectangular)	8×8×2	2 L	20×20×5
	9×9×2	2.5 L	23×23×5
	12×8×2	3 L	30×20×5
	13×9×2	3.5 L	33×23×5
Loaf Pan	8×4×3	1.5 L	20×10×7
	9×5×3	2 L	23×13×7
Round Layer Cake Pan	8×1½	1.2 L	20×4
	9×1½	1.5 L	23×4
Pie Plate	8×1¼	750 mL	20×3
	9×1¼	1 L	23×3
Baking Dish or Casserole	1 quart	1 L	—
	1½ quart	1.5 L	—
	2 quart	2 L	—